KUCHING DIARY
Peter Bialobrzeski

October 18 – October 26, 2023

Hartmann books

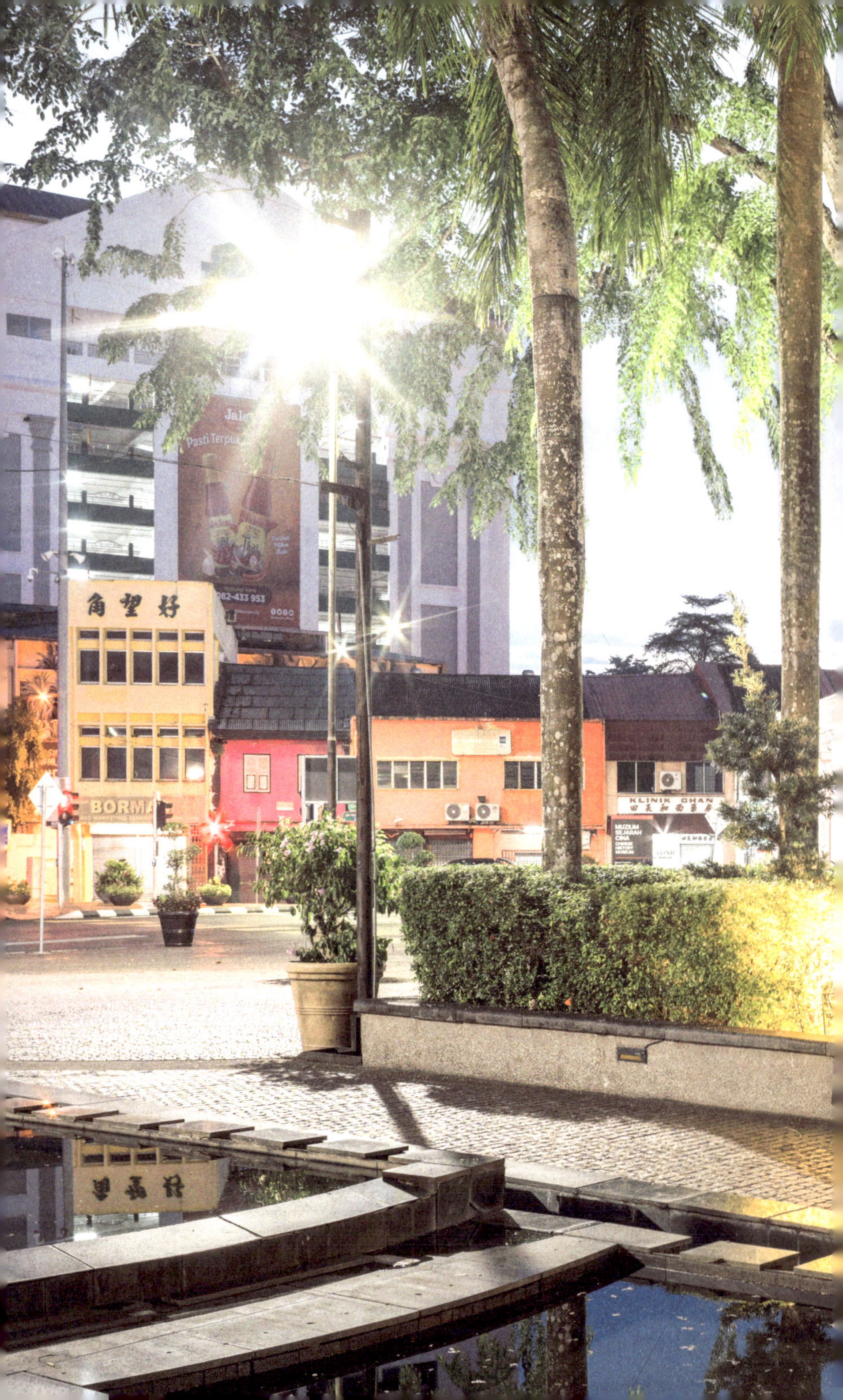
好望角
Pasti Terpu
082-433 953
BORMA
KLINIK CHAN
MUZIUM
SEJARAH
CINA
CHINESE
HISTORY
MUSEUM

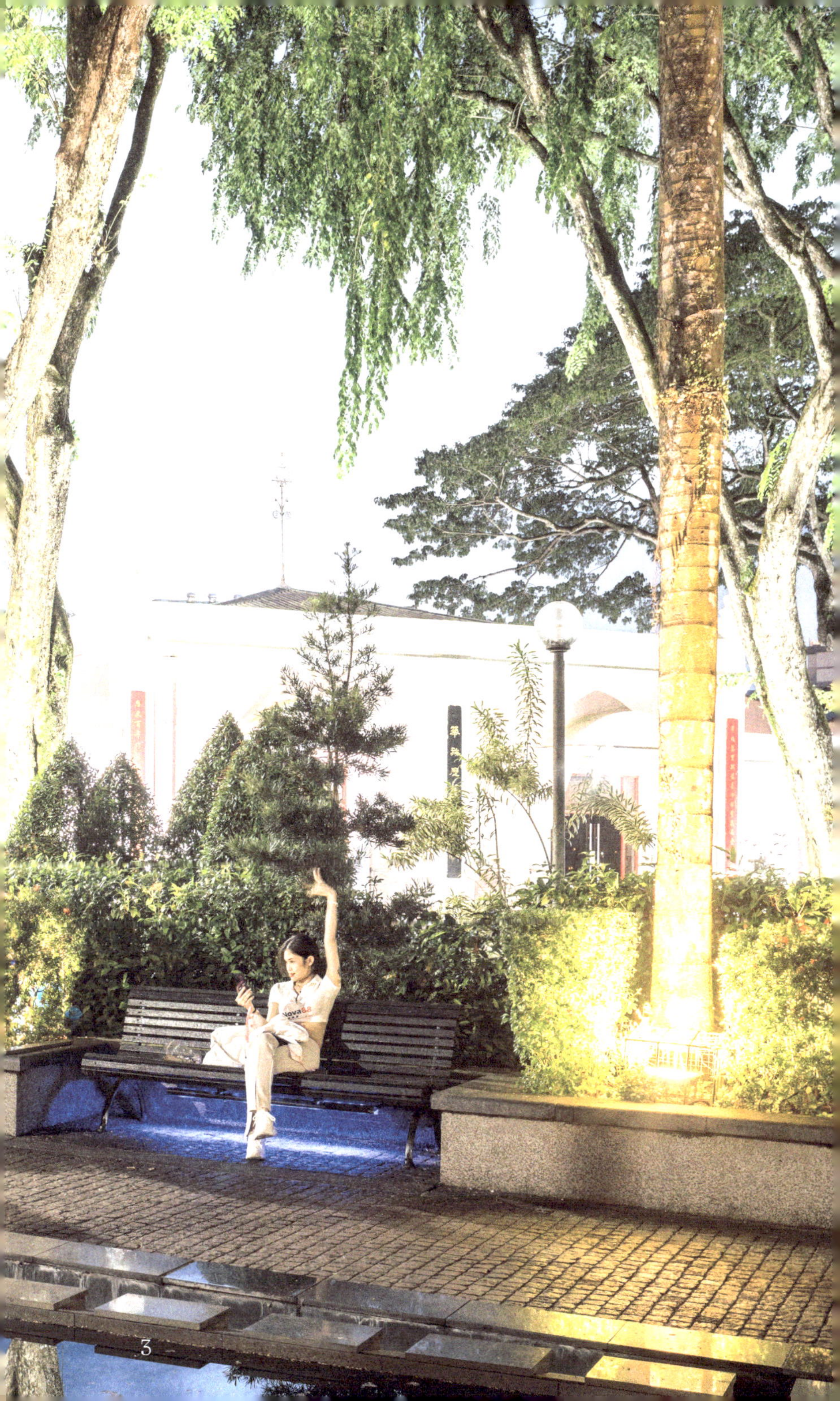

KUCHING DIARY
Peter Bialobrzeski

→October 18, 2023 The Malaysian Meteorological Department issued a thunderstorm warning for Kuching and other areas in southern Sarawak this morning—and yes, the rain is pouring down. First observation apart from that: unlike I was told, the city is not that quiet. On the contrary, during rush hour hardly anybody walks. Instead, fourwheelers dominate the streets, and traffic lights are rare. Pedestrians, beware!
→October 19, 2023 Sarawak police conducted *Ops Tapis Kahs*, which does not translate well into English, but resulted in the arrest of five young adults, including a seventeen-year-old teenage girl, for possession of more than forty kilos of methamphetamine. Until 2022 the teens would have faced the death penalty, but now the judge has the option of sentencing the offenders to forty years in prison.
→October 20, 2023 Around the city you will see the name James Brooke on almost every corner. This notorious Englishman, known as Sarawak's white rajah, was an inspiration for Joseph Conrad's fiction. Moviegoers may recognize a colonel living upstream on the Mekong. Unlike Kurtz, Brooke was appointed rajah by the sultan of Brunei—colonialism with Indigenous support—proof that the abuse of power is not limited to skin color or birthplace.
→October 21, 2023 I learn from the German media that Malaysia has withdrawn from the Frankfurt Book Fair, which is taking place this week, due to my country's support of Israel. On the street, I experience open smiles wherever I go, even from women wearing hijabs. The neighboring state police chief Datuk Jauteh Dikun, according to *The Borneo Post*, comments: "The Sabah police advise any party not to raise religious issues if they are not qualified and knowledgeable about it, especially if it is not their religion." →October 22, 2023 It seems obligatory that a thunderstorm hits the city every day. For the occasion of the week, small white tents have been set up along the banks of the river. I was expecting some kind of festival, but except for a *Led Zeppelin* cover band that kept me awake at night, it never happened. The night ends with the fajr prayers from the mosque on the other side of the river, just before sunrise. To keep the Western visitor from falling asleep again, it is sometimes followed by a long, loudspeaker-transmitted sermon by the imam. *The Borneo Post* reports that a certain Pli Lee shared a photo of

the colorful carcass of a rare jambu fruit dove on Facebook. An unidentified tour guide is quoted: "This is one of the examples of what can happen when birds have to fly through the cityscape and along buildings that are not equipped with features to prevent birds from crashing into them." → October 23, 2023 Lunch at a Western café: the menu advertises a *keto meal* as a healthy alternative. Instead of rice, a mix of shredded cauliflower and tapioca leaves is served with a deep-fried chicken leg. The high-fat, low-carbohydrate balance may only be disturbed by the cocktail of antibiotics, steroids, and greasy cooking oil inside the chicken thigh. Again, as always on this side of the world, I prefer to eat local, sit on plastic chairs by the river, and not be bothered by Western hipster prose on the menu. → October 24, 2023 Roaming around the city, I wonder why so few people are walking. The answer is that there are plenty of parking spaces for cars—literally everyone is driving their air-conditioned vehicles. The infrastructure makes walking rather unpleasant, the city is noisy, streets are difficult to cross, and the friendly inhabitants of Kuching are only to be found in restaurants and shopping malls.

→ October 25, 2023 Today is the opening of the Science Film Festival. A selection of films, all dealing with environmental issues, will be screened at the Sarawak State Library auditorium. Concerns about the planet are expressed, supported by a UN program, while viewers are shocked by an overambitious air-conditioning policy. Did I mention that the library—like most places in Kuching—can only be reached by car? Apart from an excessively advertised electric bus that runs hourly to circumnavigate the city, there is no public transport to speak of. → October 26, 2023 Across the river in the Sarawak state assembly, a member of parliament named Mordi Bimol is speaking out strongly against the ministry of education's launch of a Palestine solidarity week in schools. Bimol explains his position: "Promote unity, refrain from division. Promote harmony, refrain from war. Promote respect, refrain from conflict. Promote compassion, refrain from hatred. Promote tolerance, refrain from selfishness. Promote sustainability, refrain from destruction." I can only agree before I take a *Grab* to the airport.

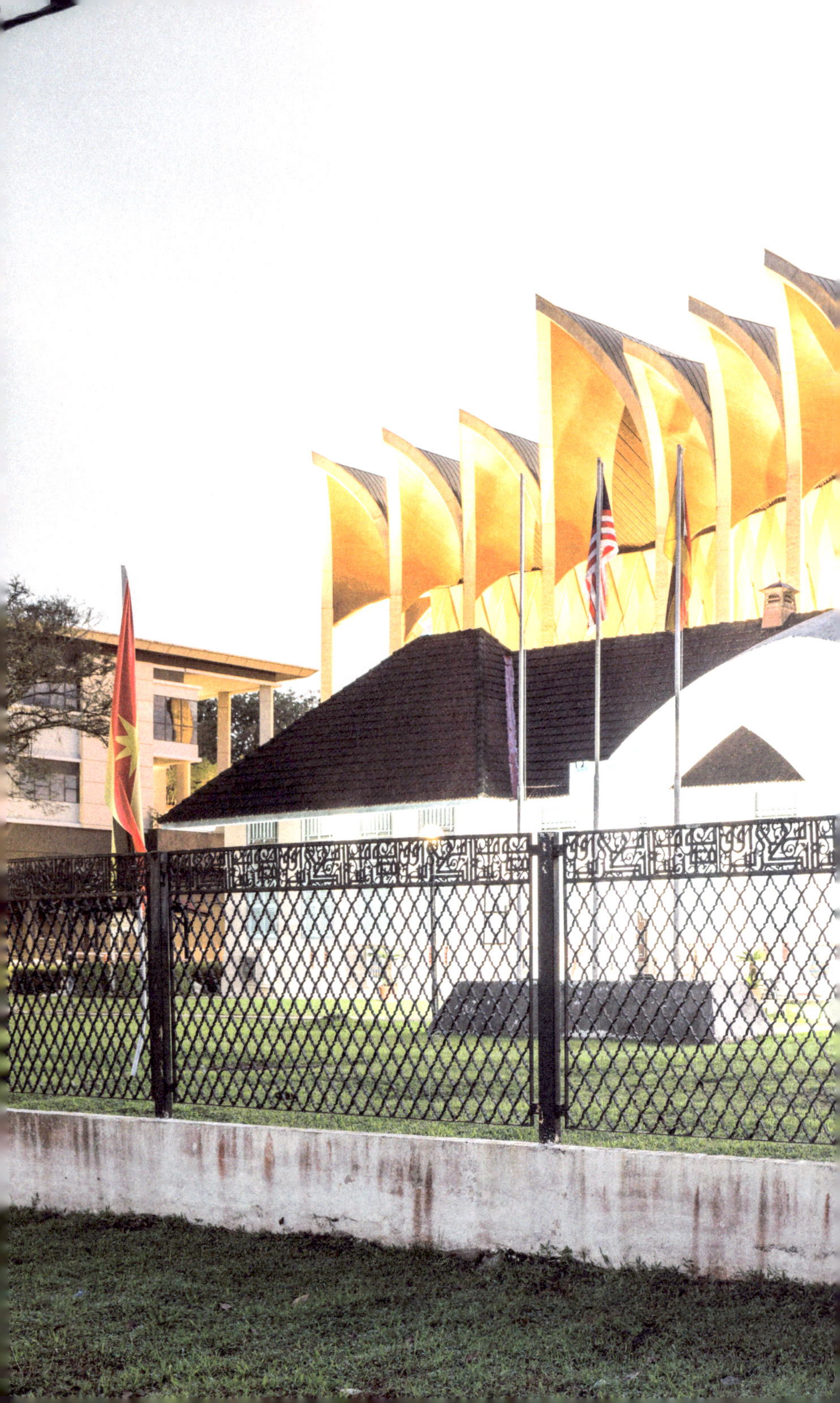

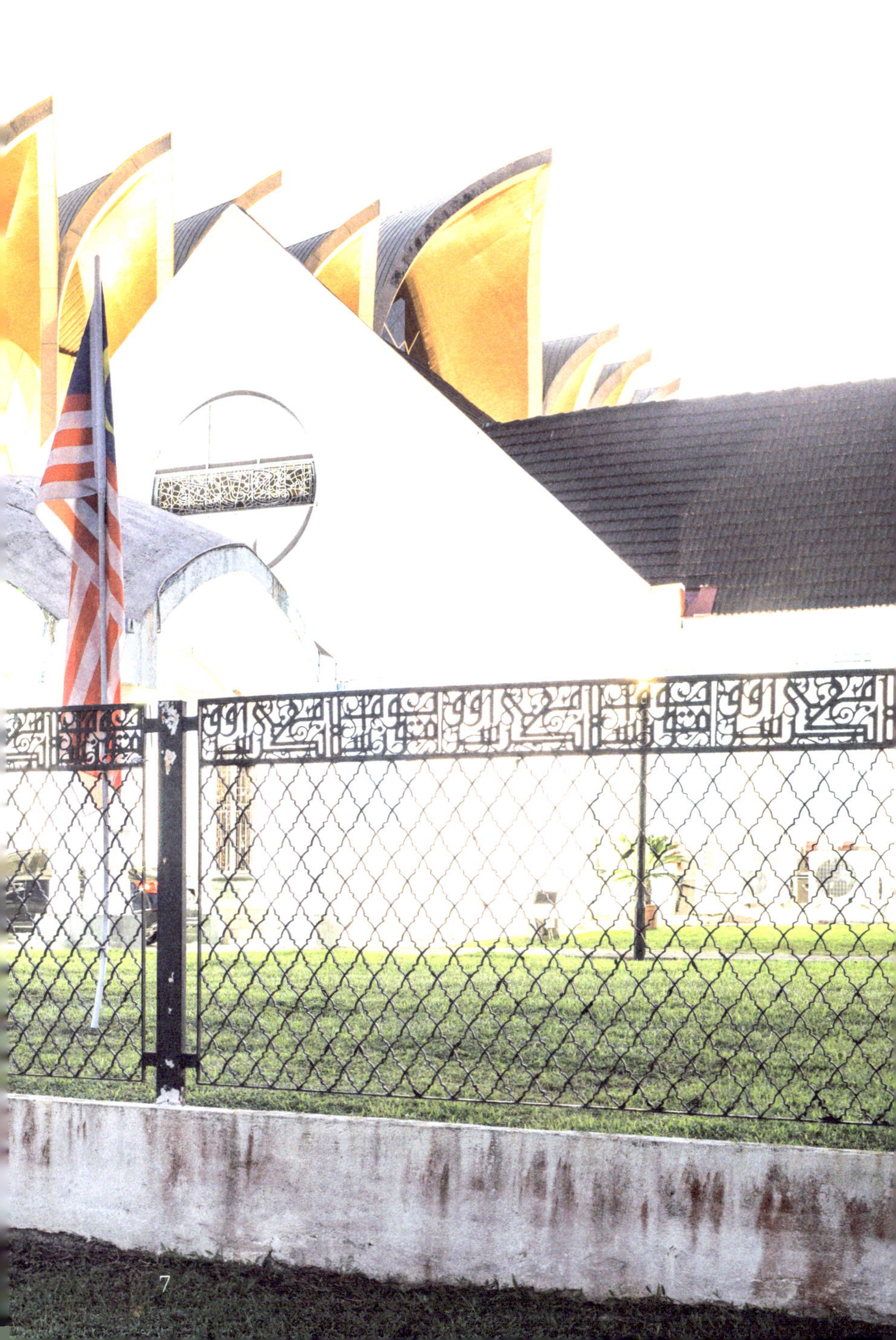

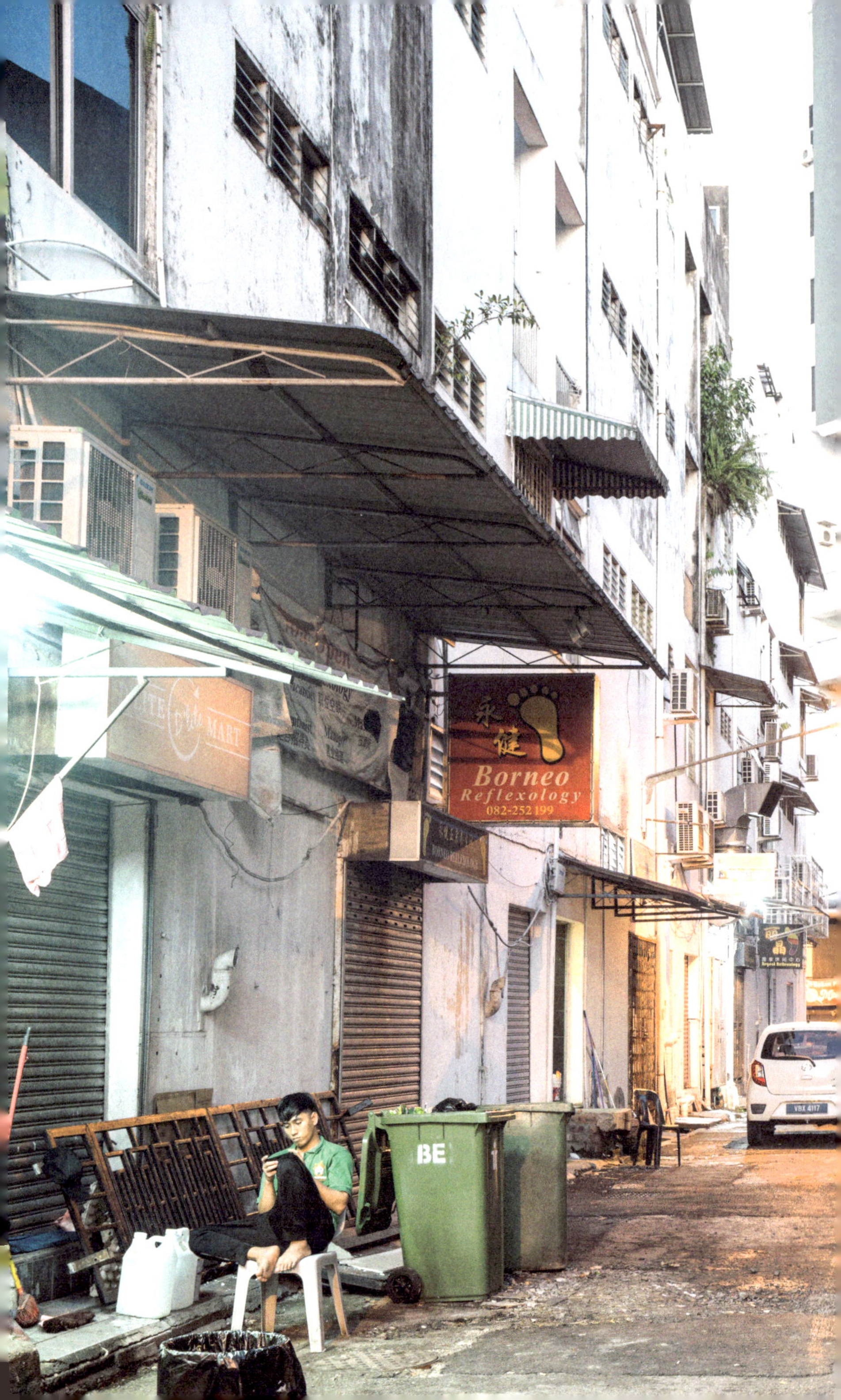

永健
Borneo
Reflexology
082-252 199
MART
BE
VBX 4117

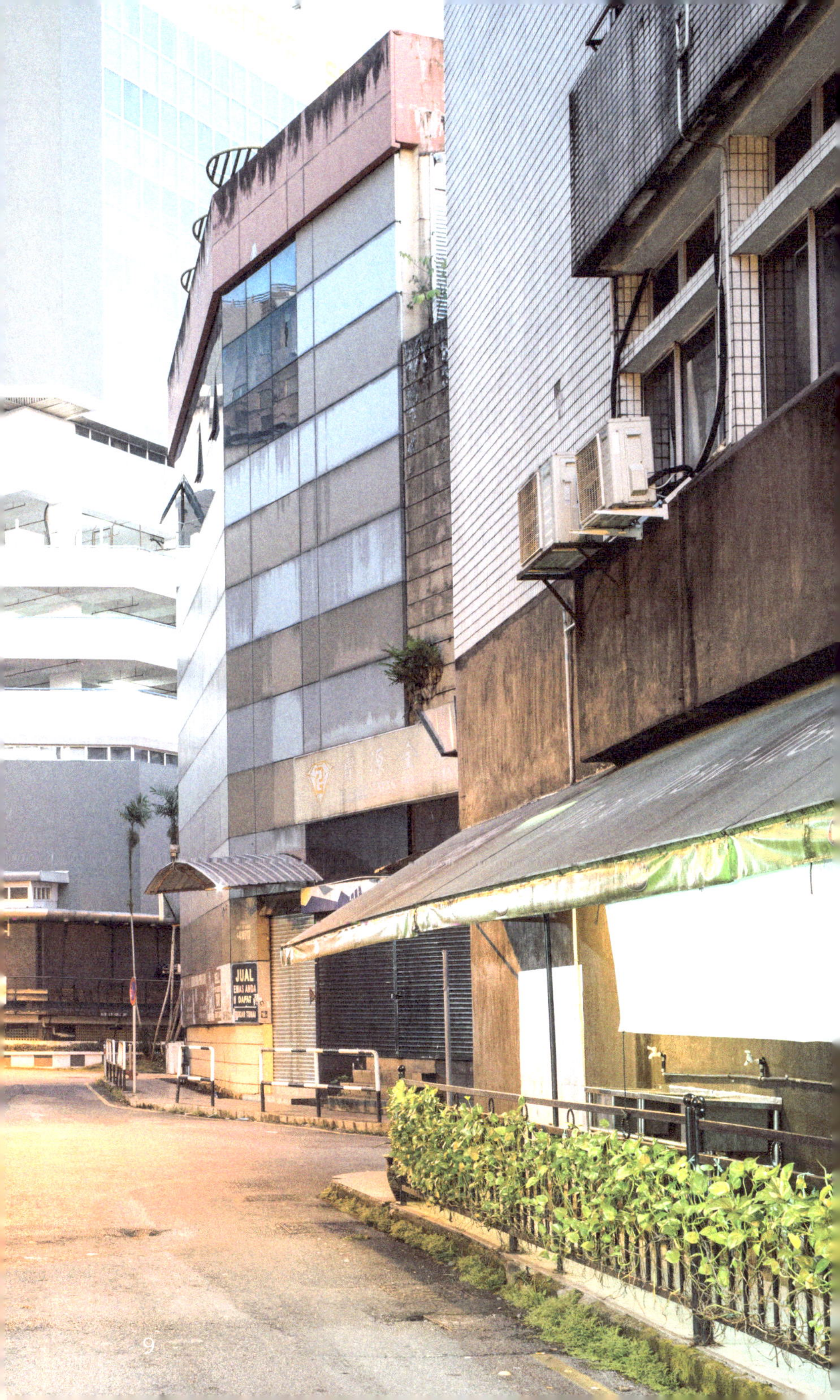
JUAL
EMAS ANDA

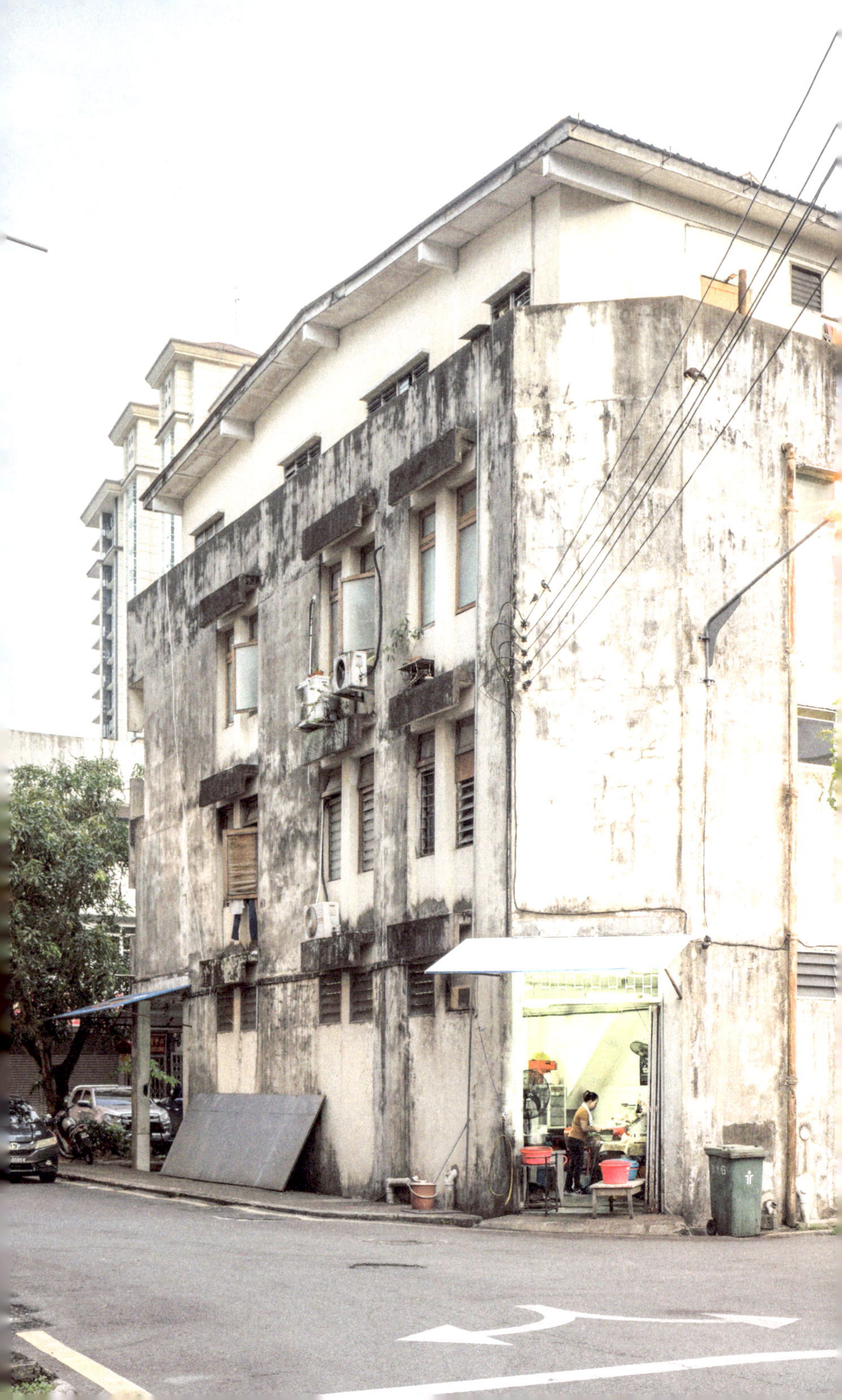

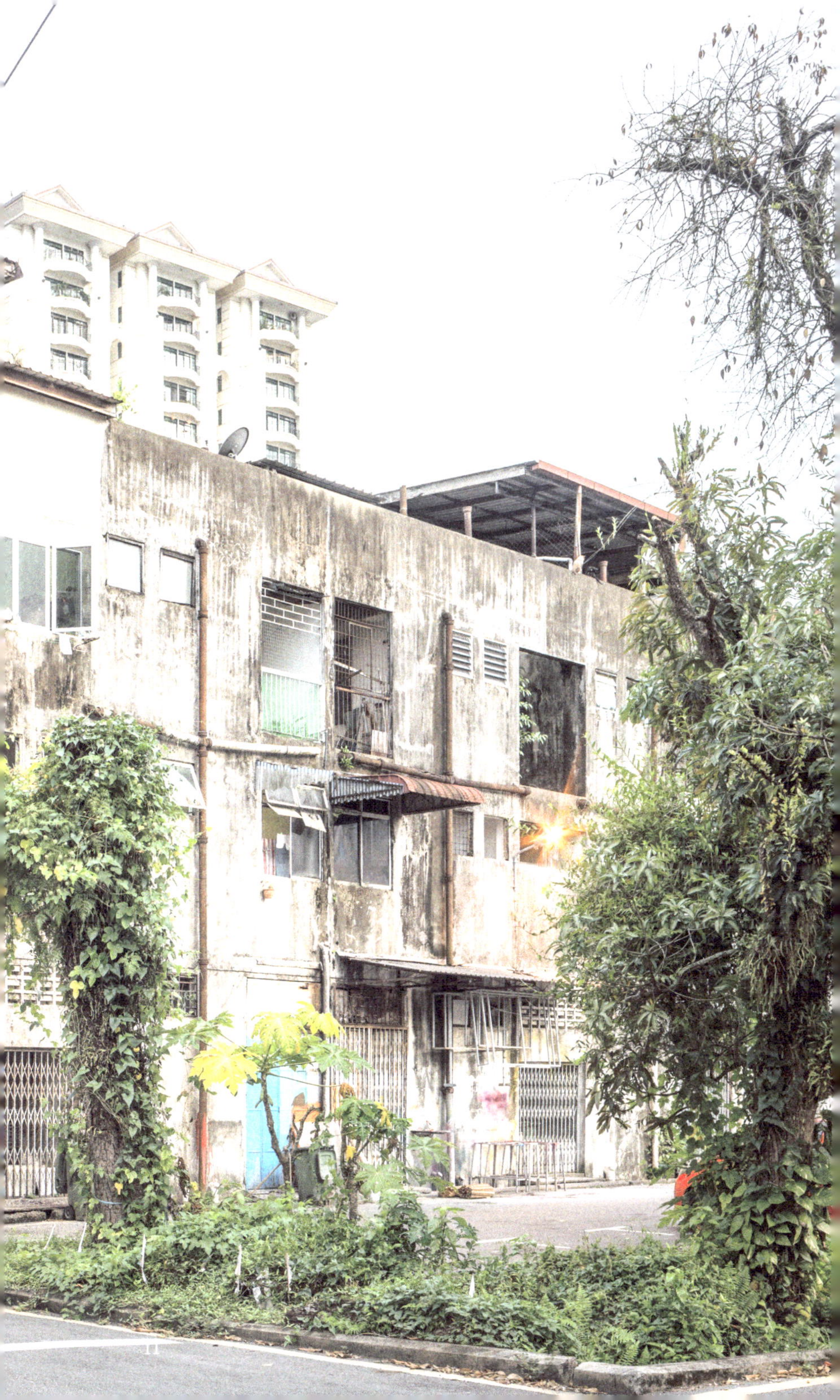

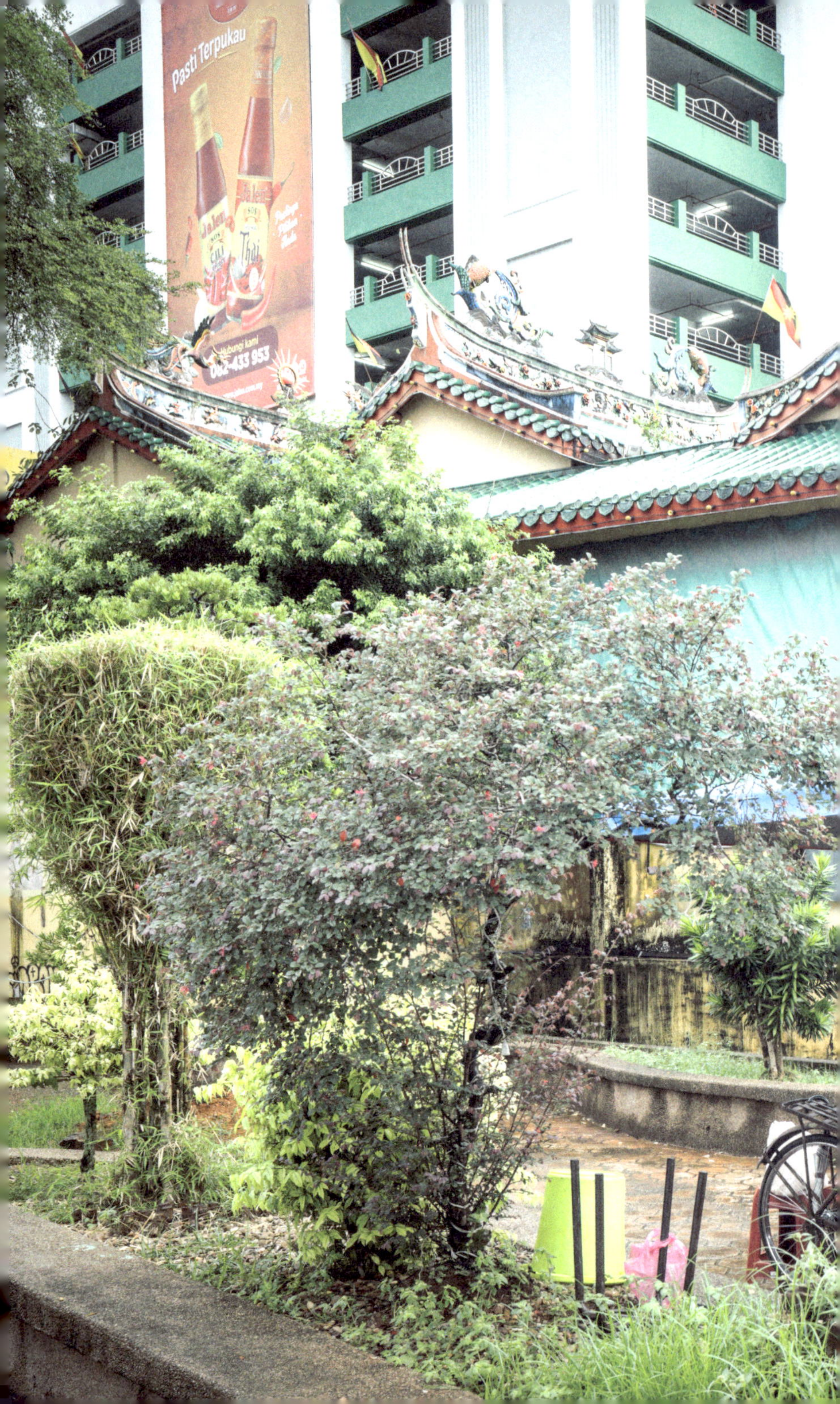
Pasti Terpukau
Thai
Hubungi kami
082-433 953

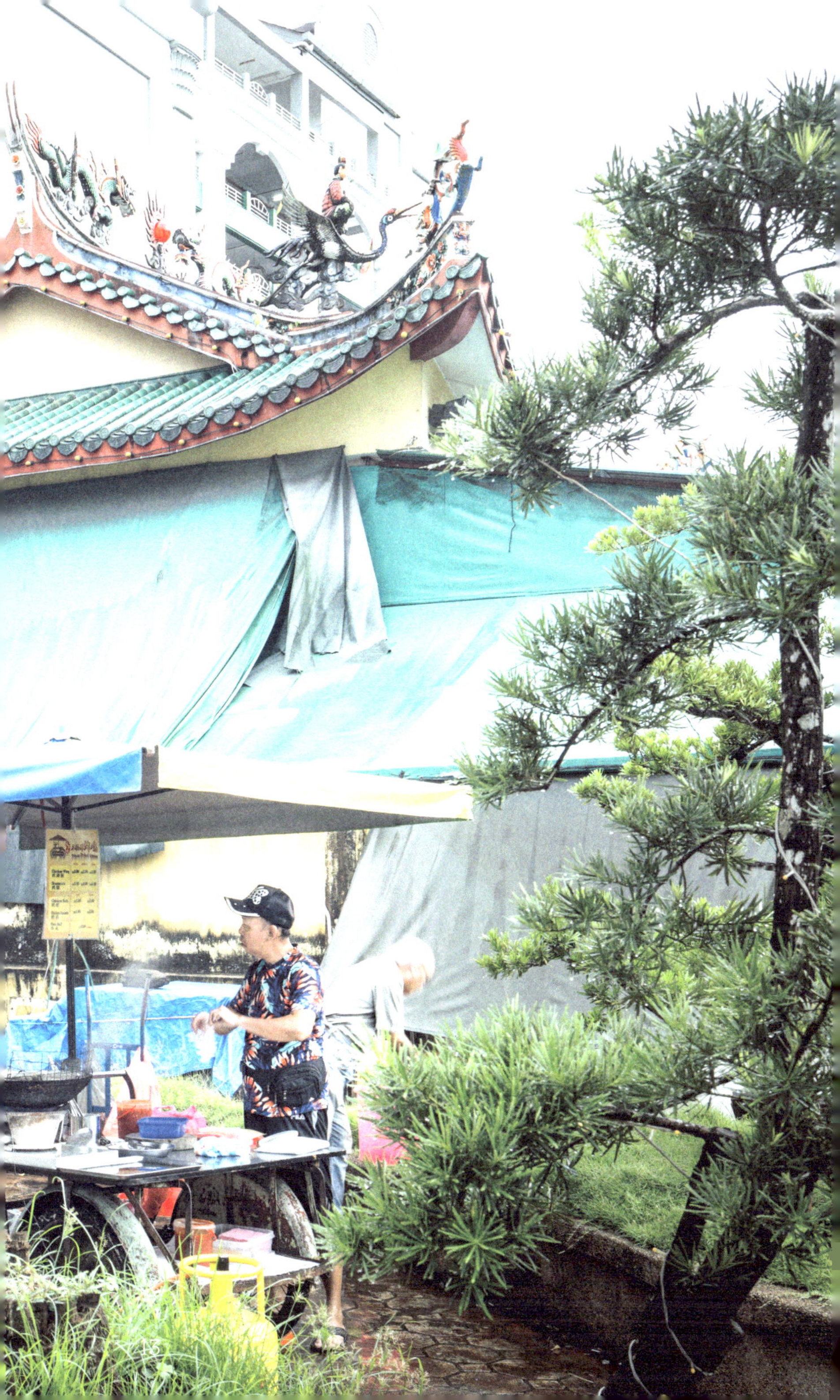

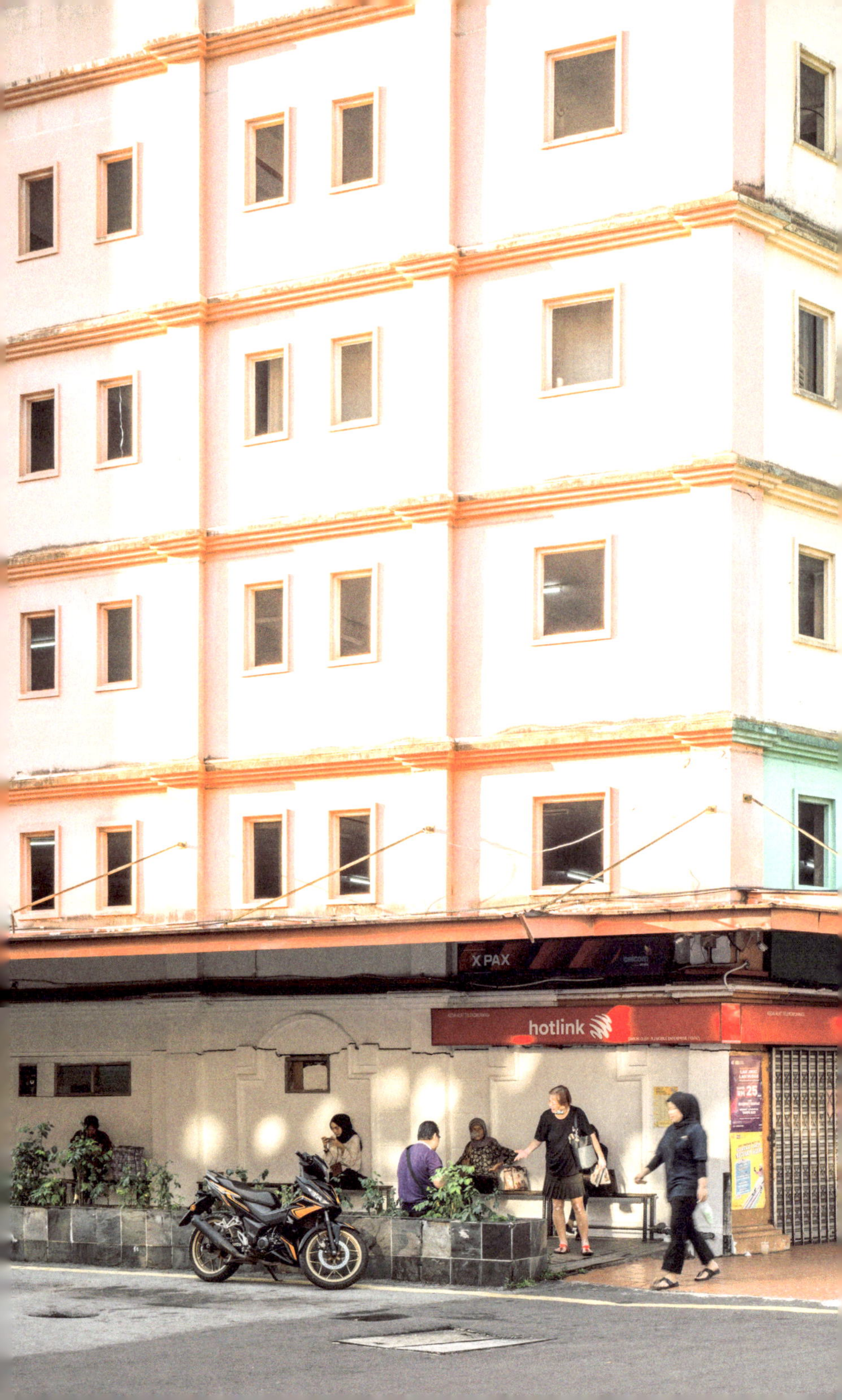
X PAX
hotlink

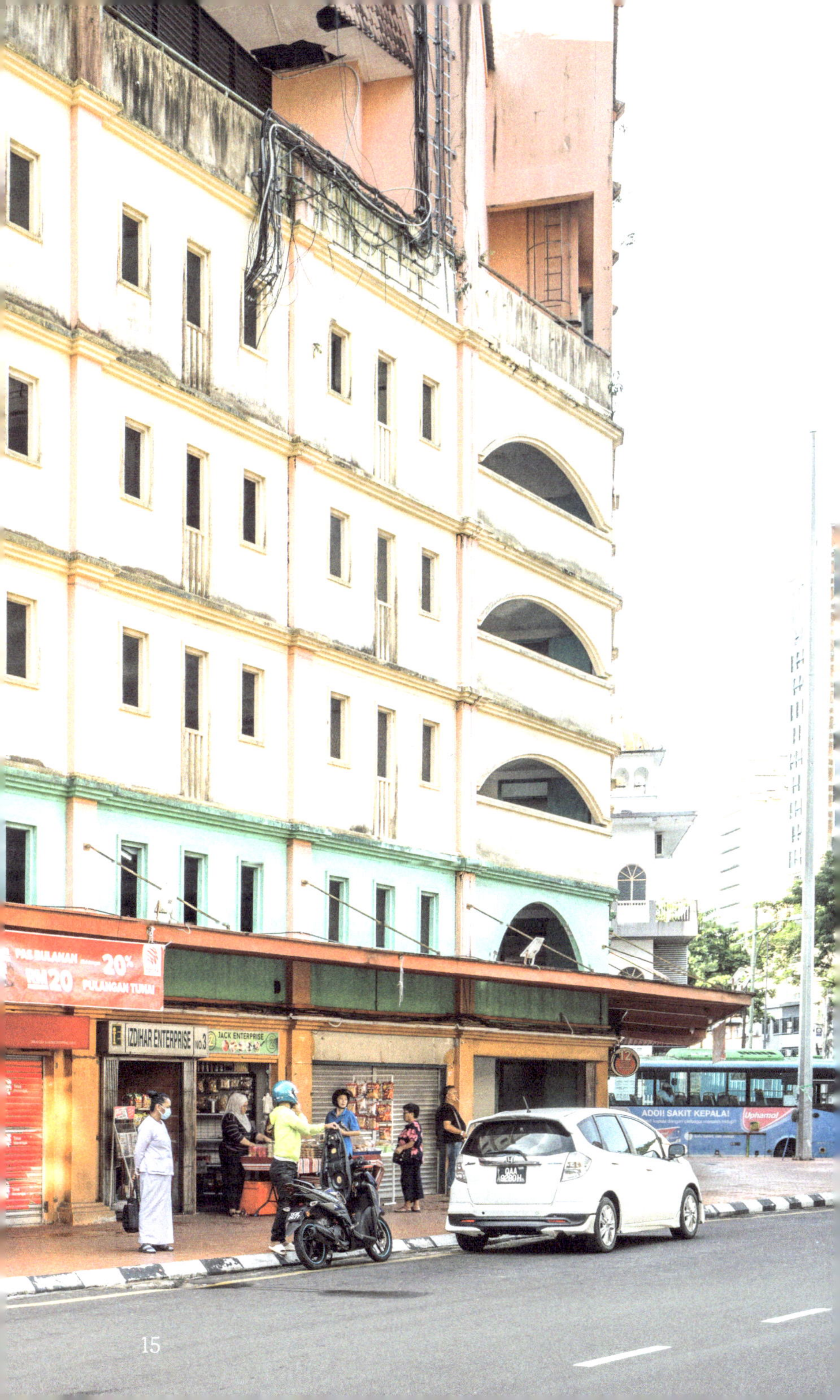
20%
RM20
PULANGAN TUNAI
IZDIHAR ENTERPRISE No.3
JACK ENTERPRISE
ADOI! SAKIT KEPALA!
Uphamol

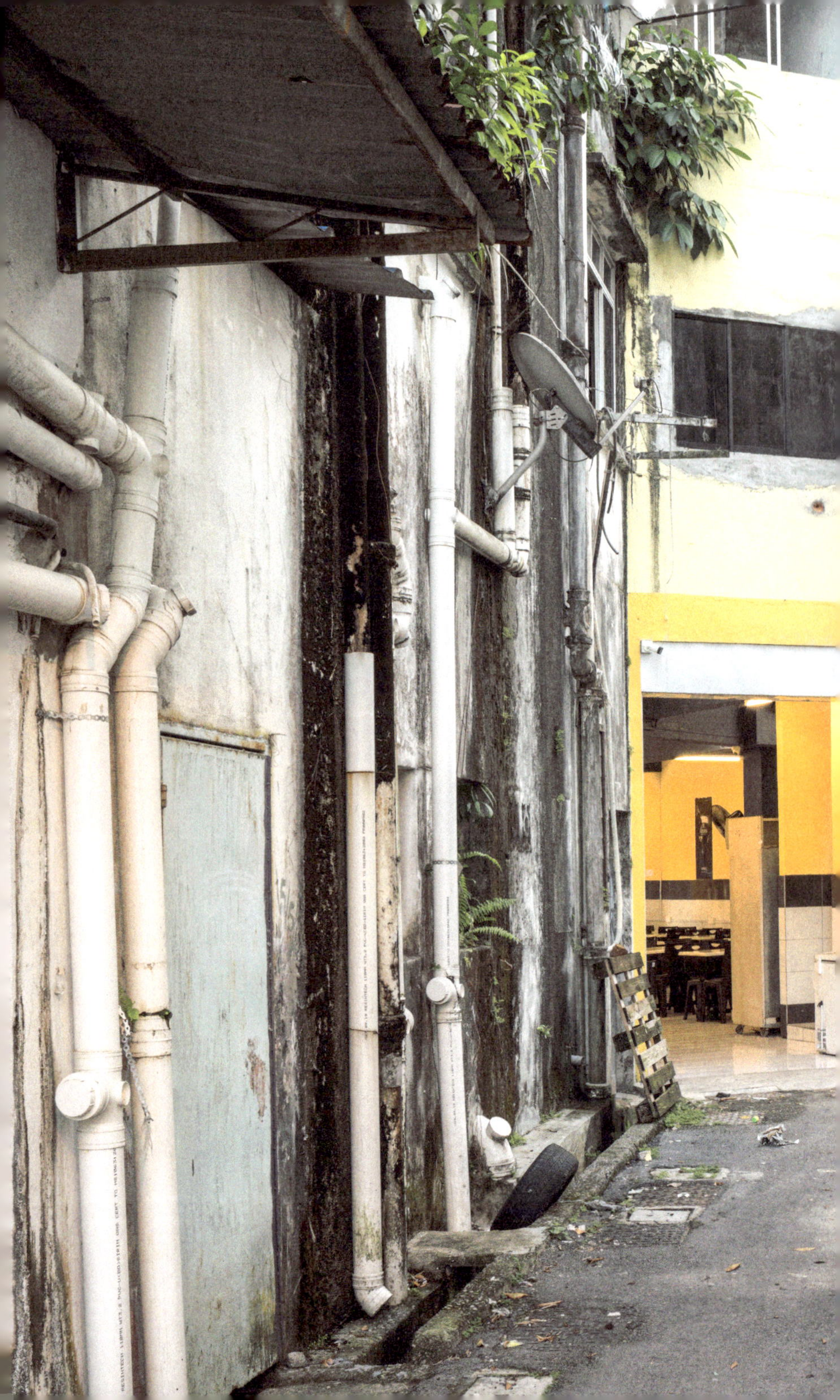

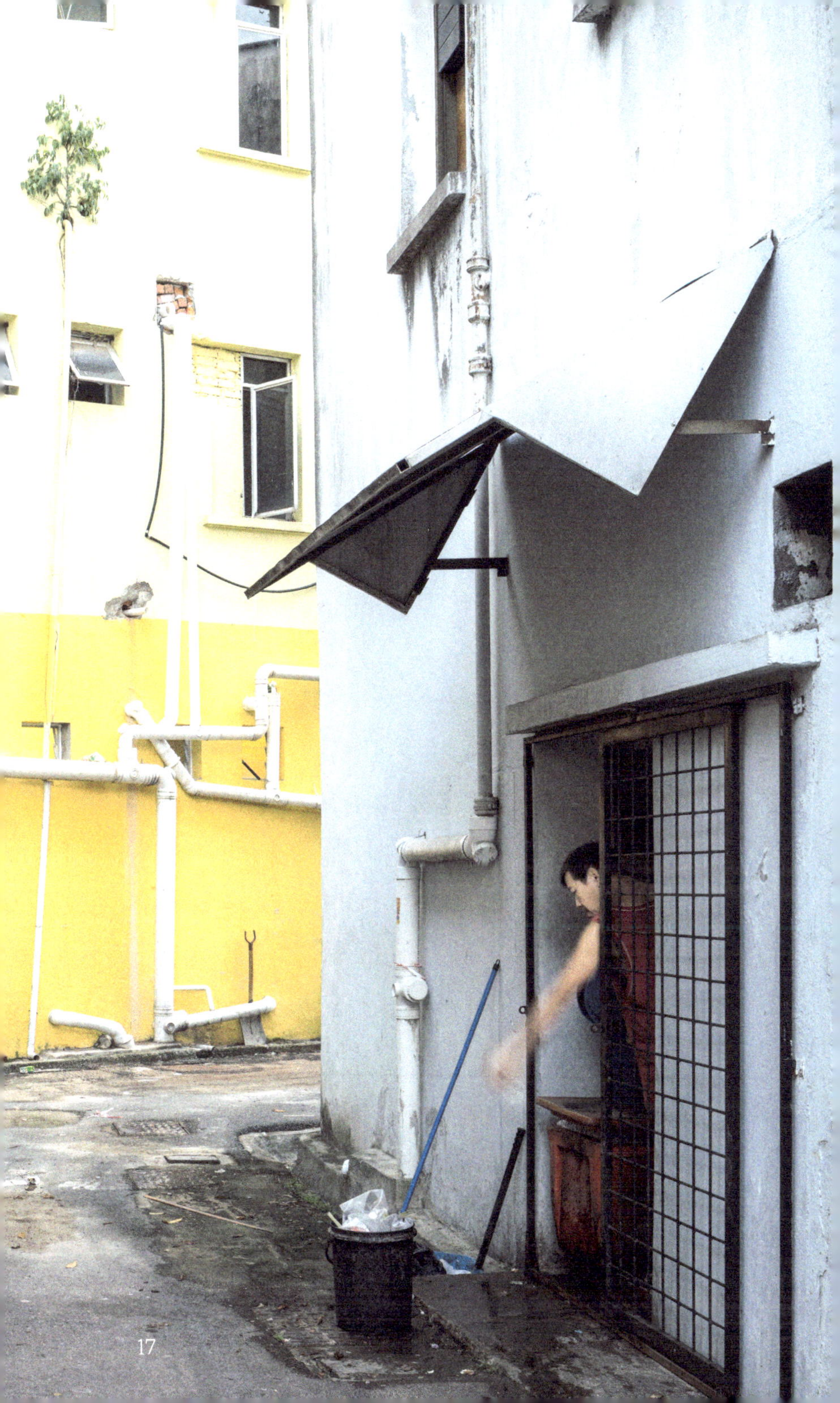

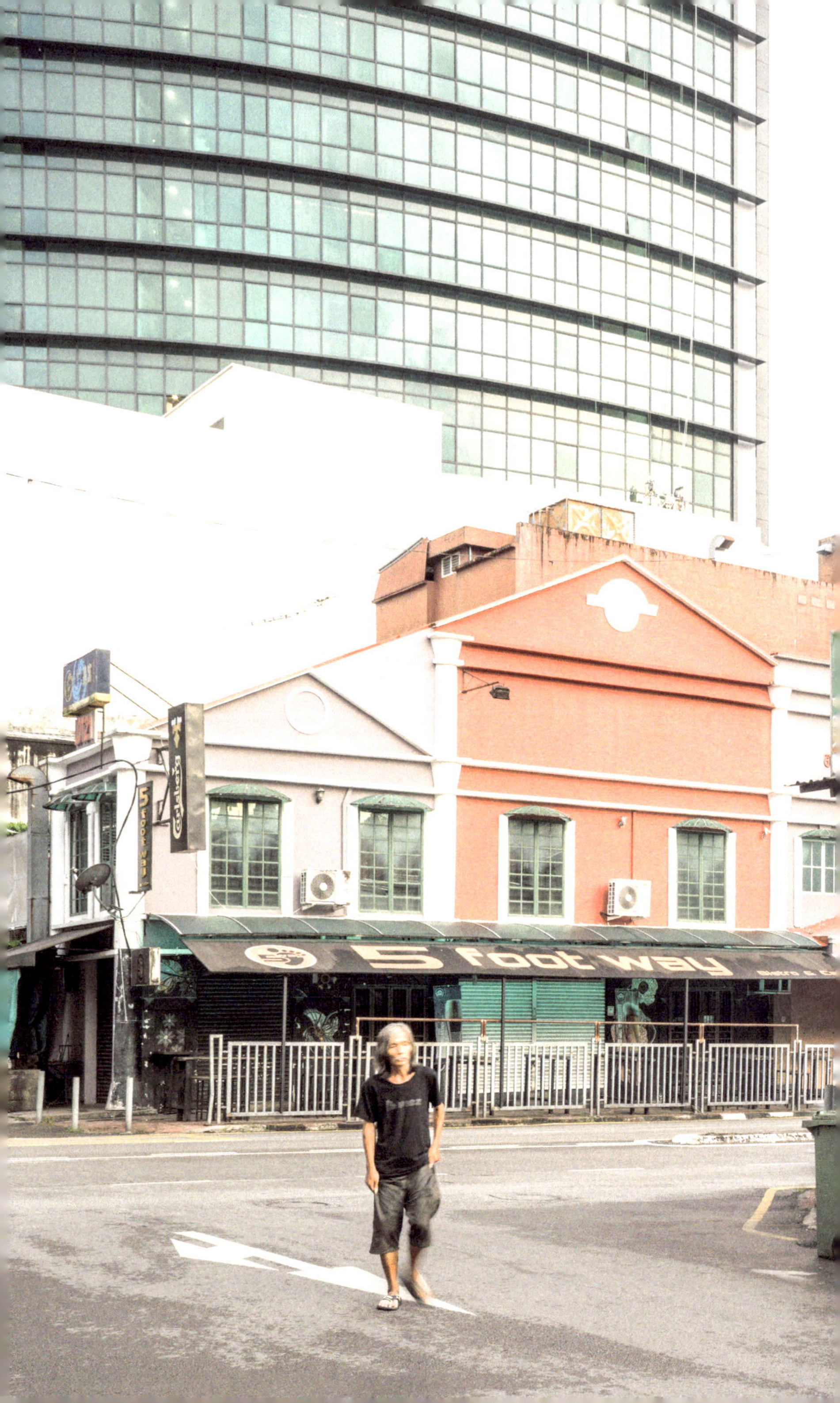
5 foot way

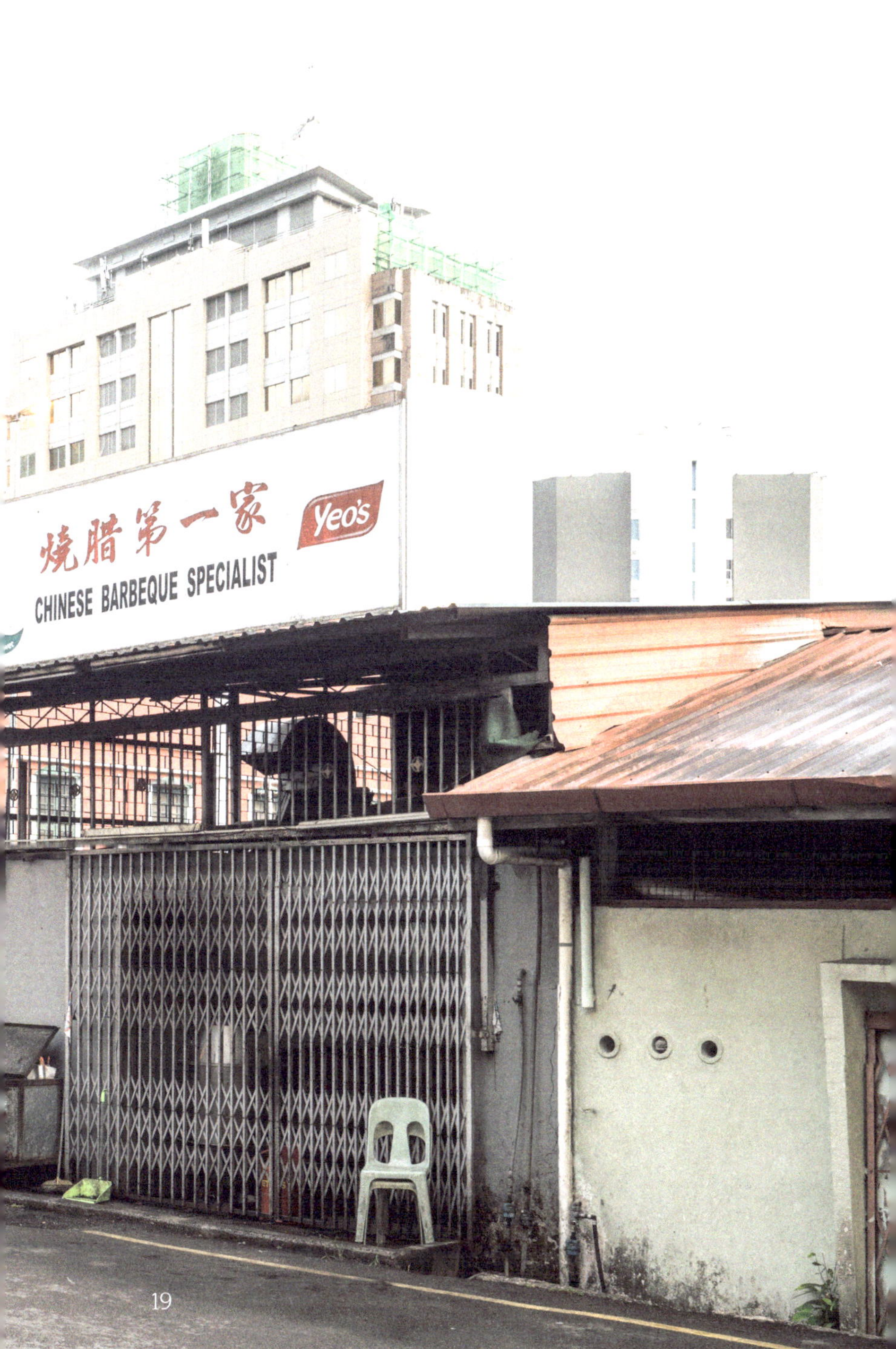
烧腊第一家
Yeo's
CHINESE BARBEQUE SPECIALIST

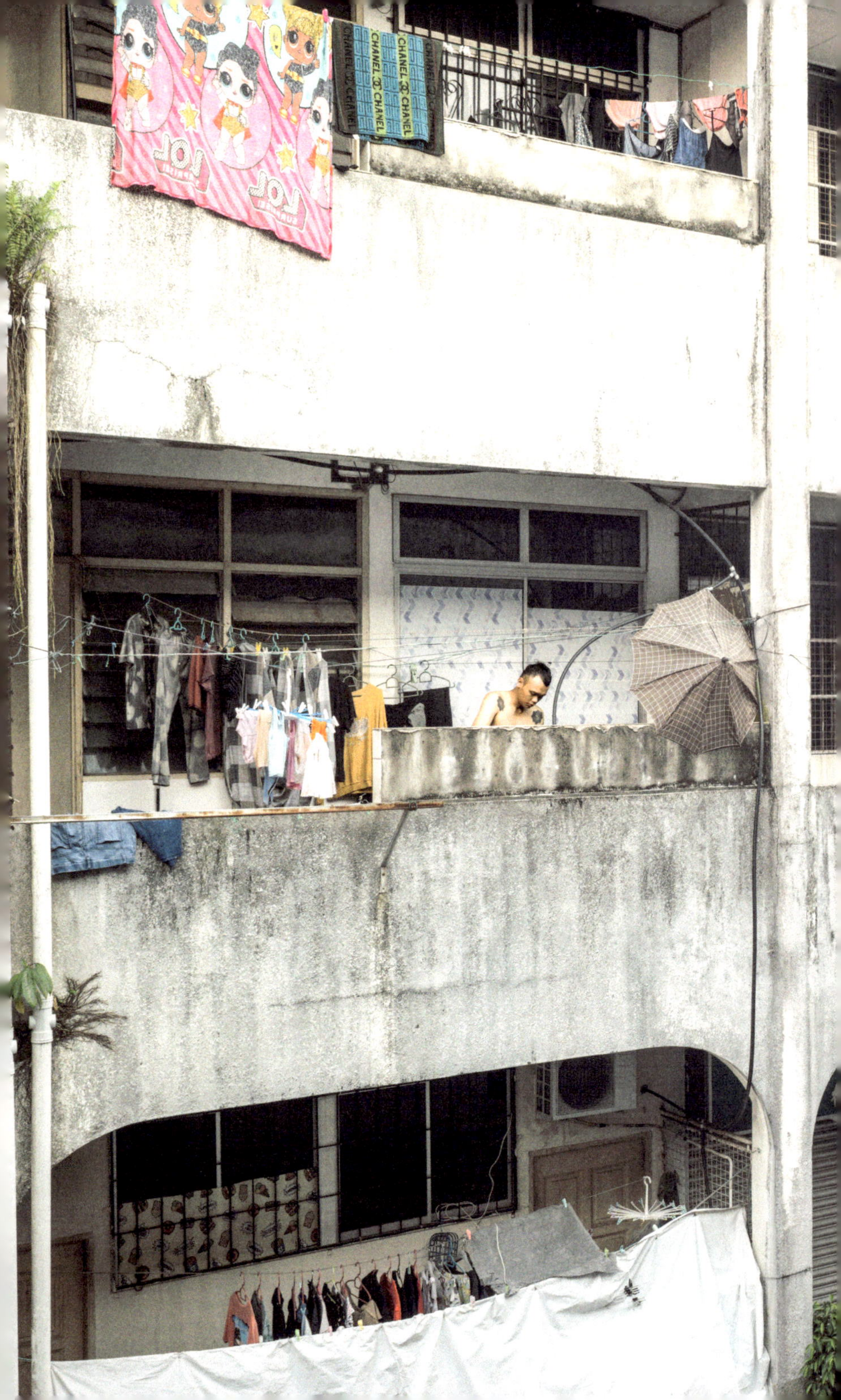
LOL
CHANEL

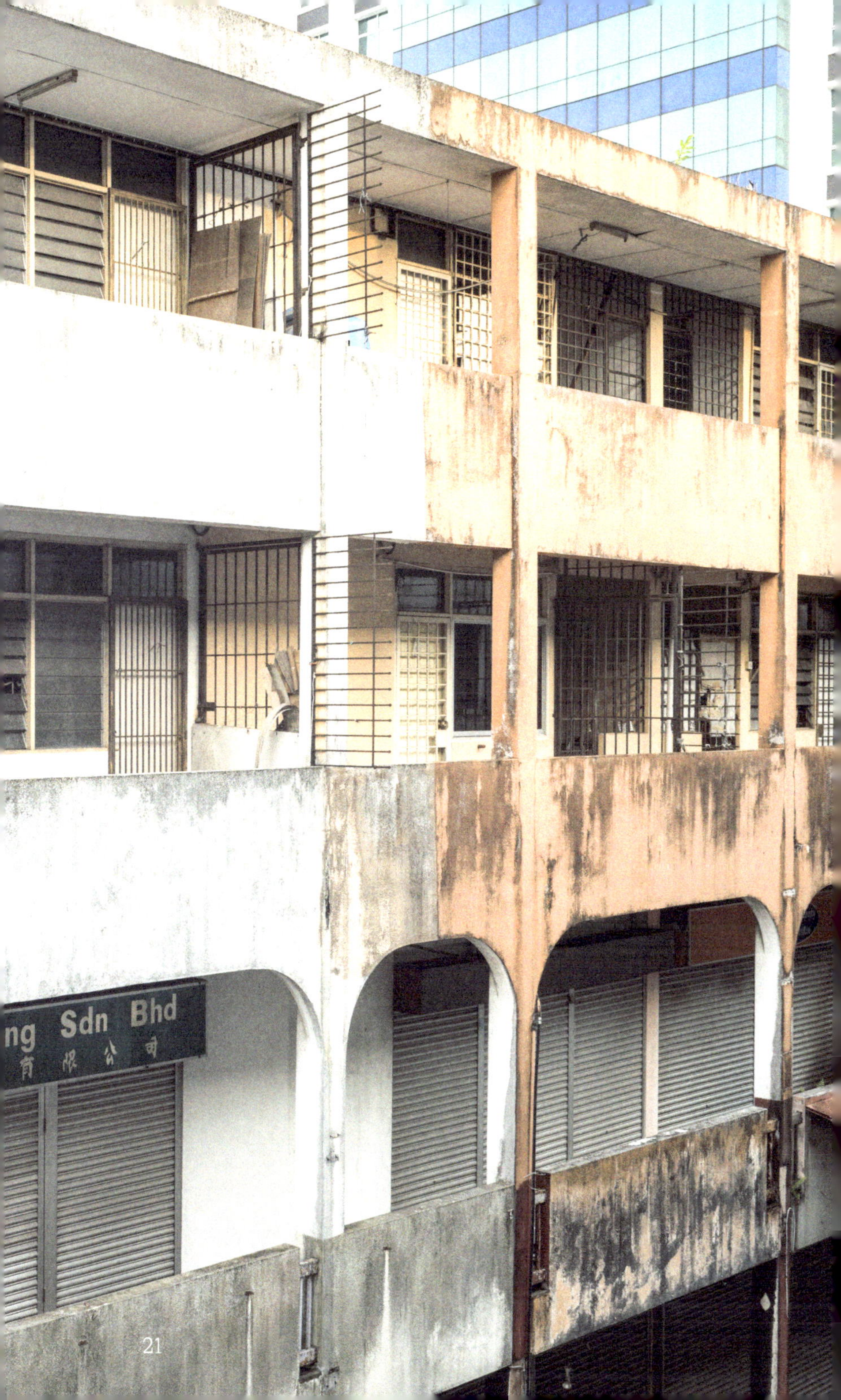
ng Sdn Bhd
有限公司

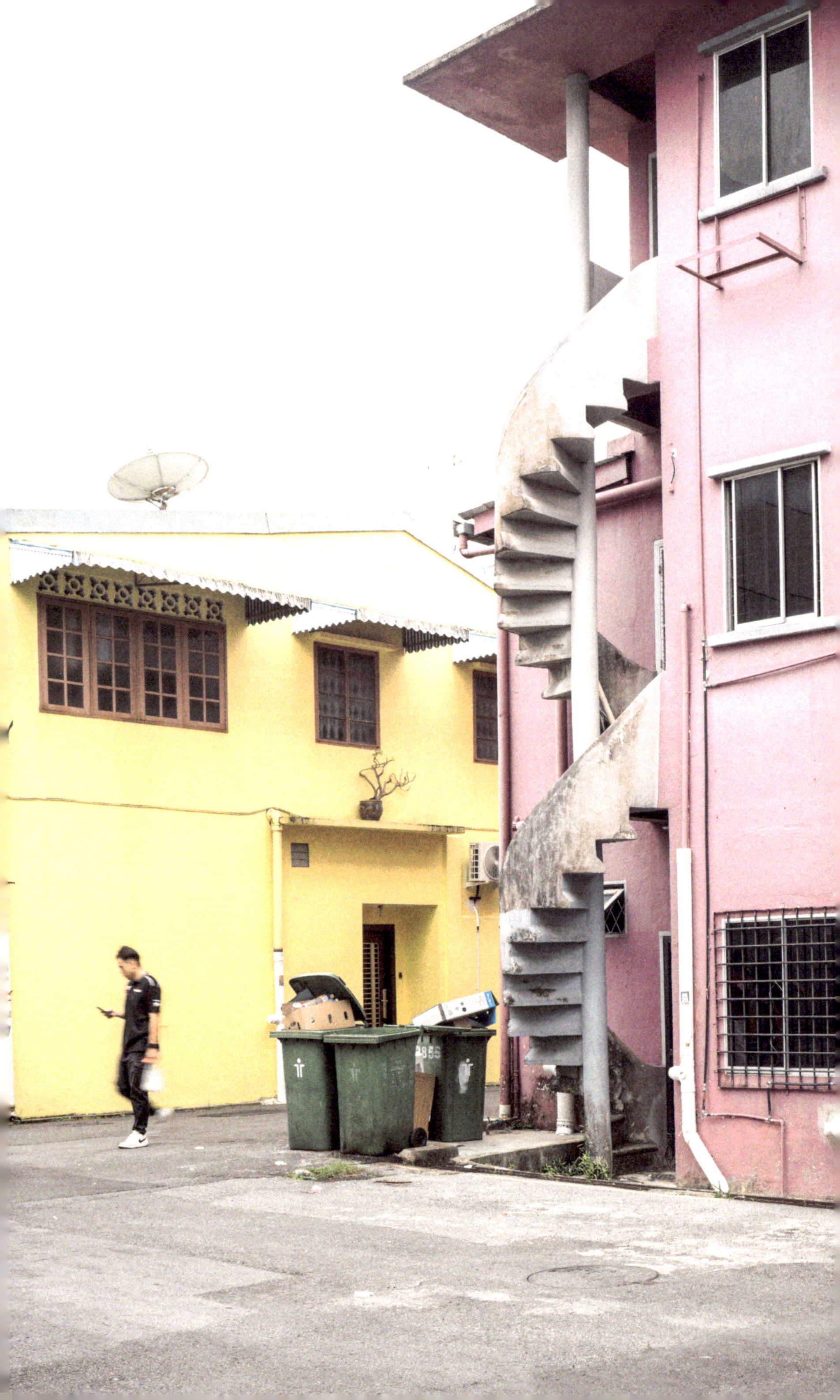

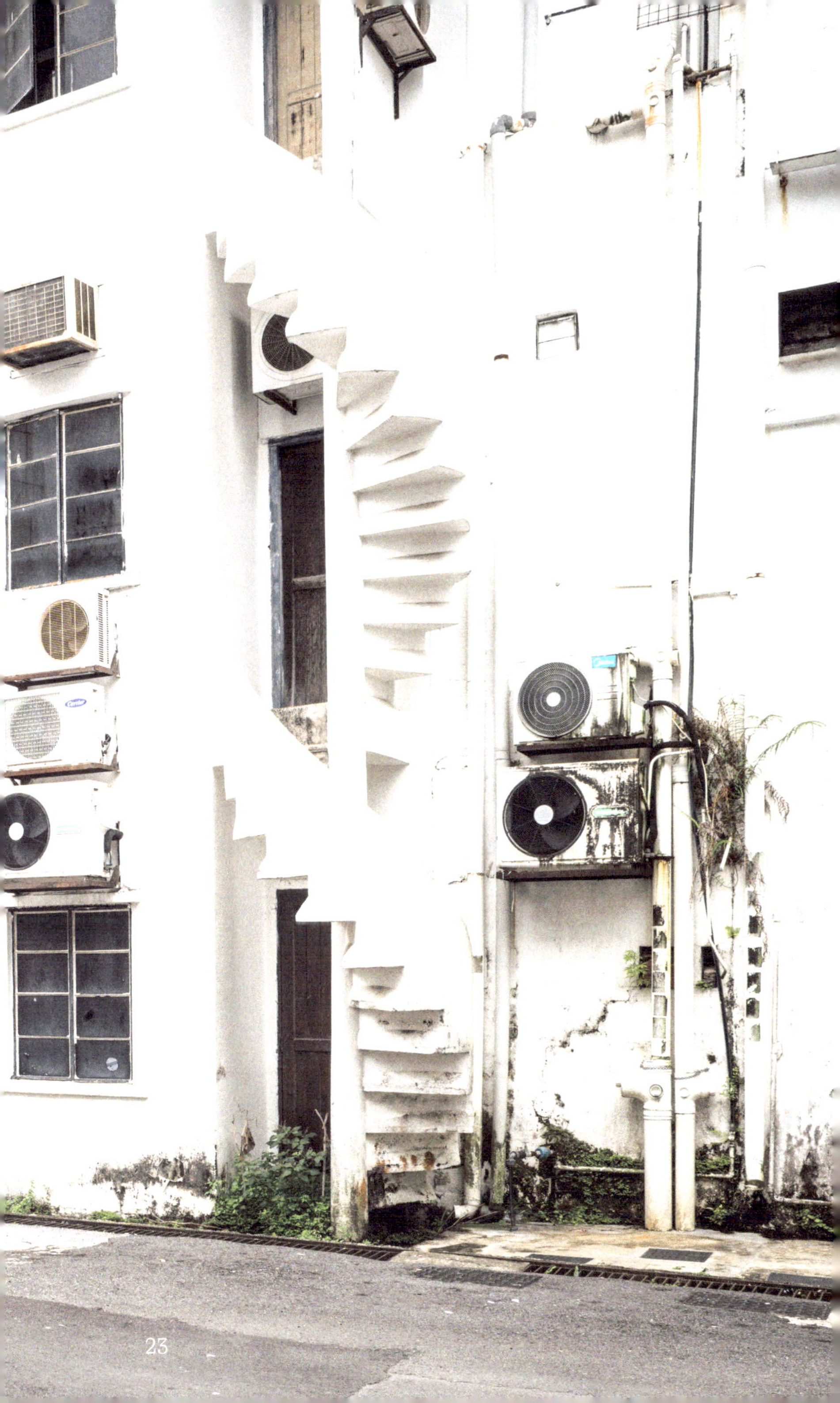

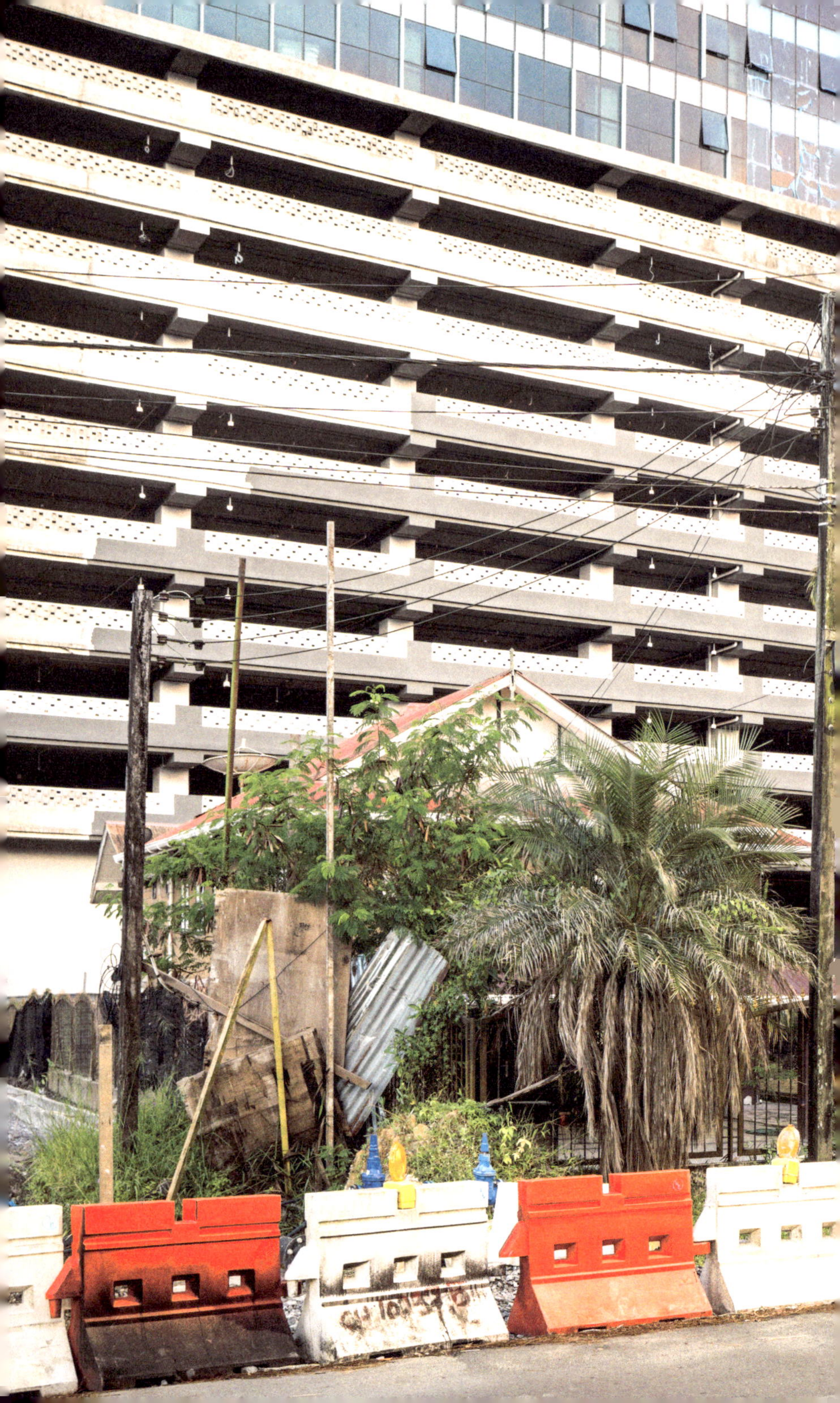

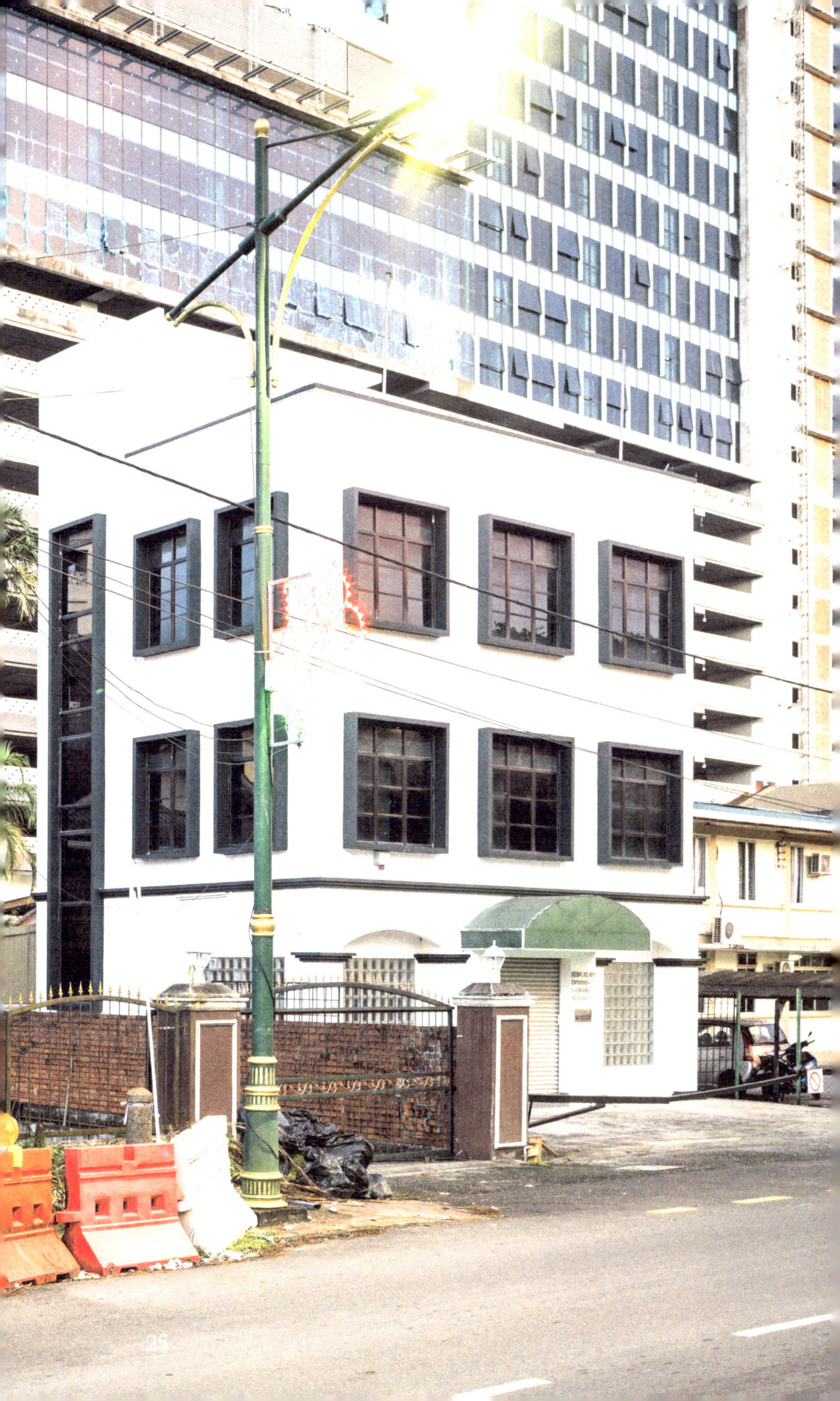

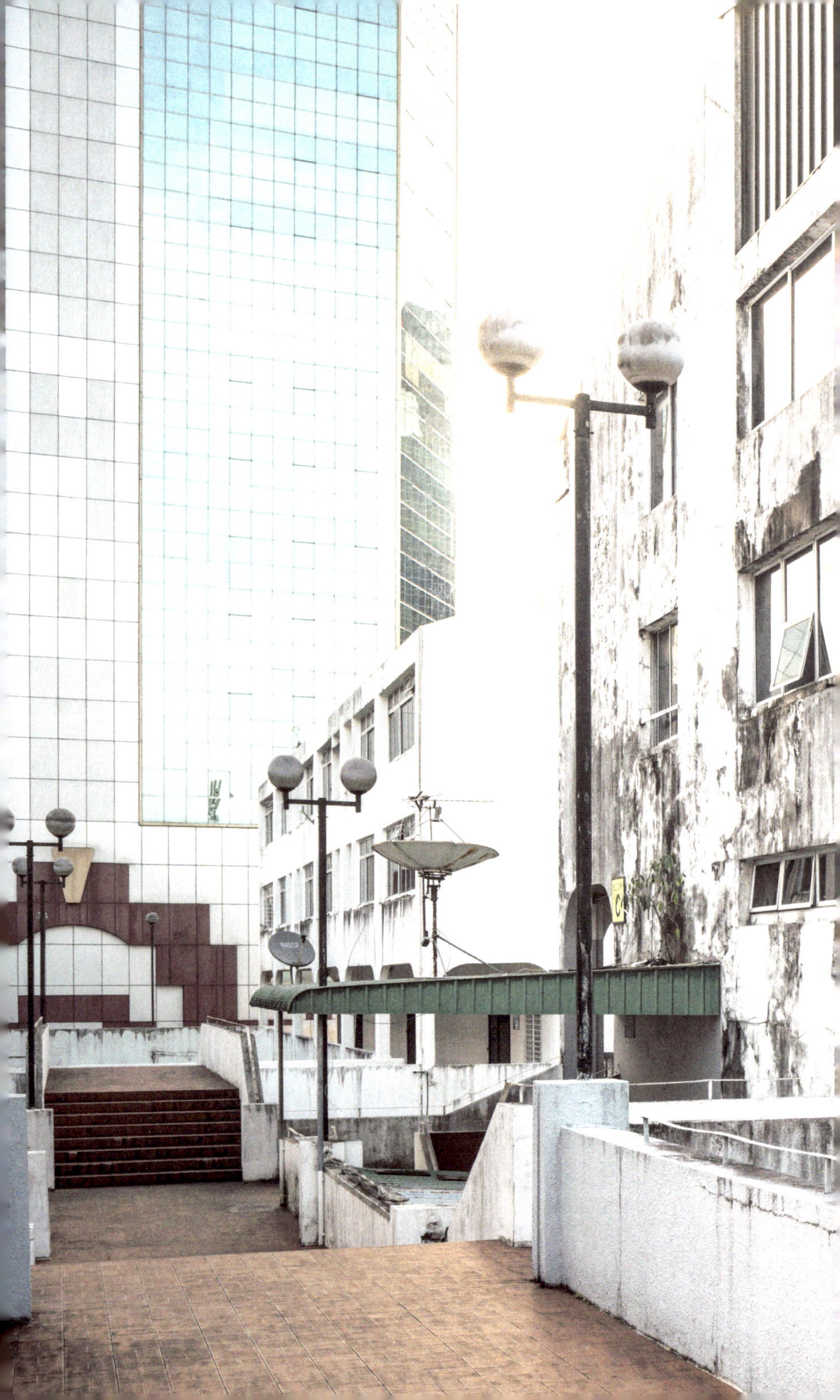

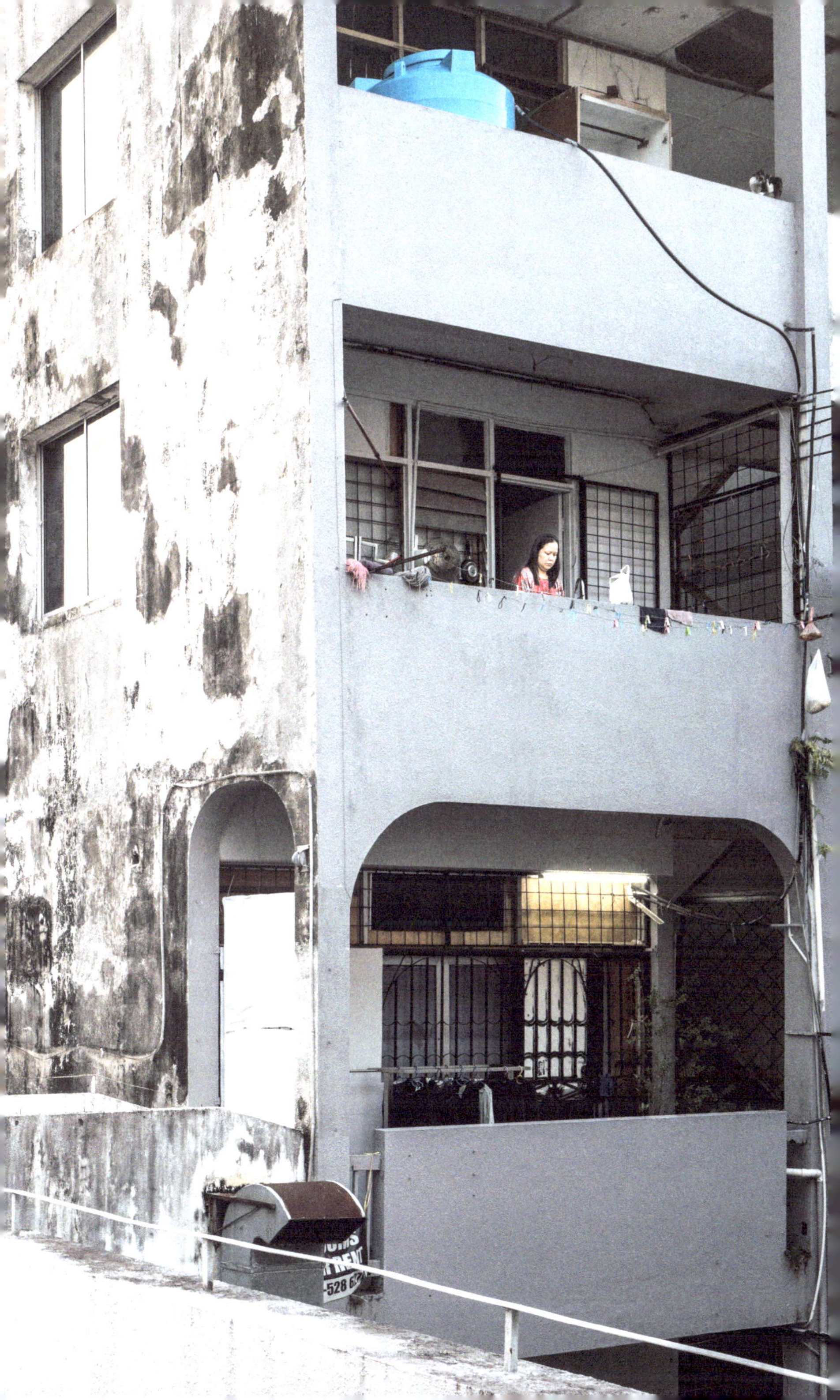
RENT
-528

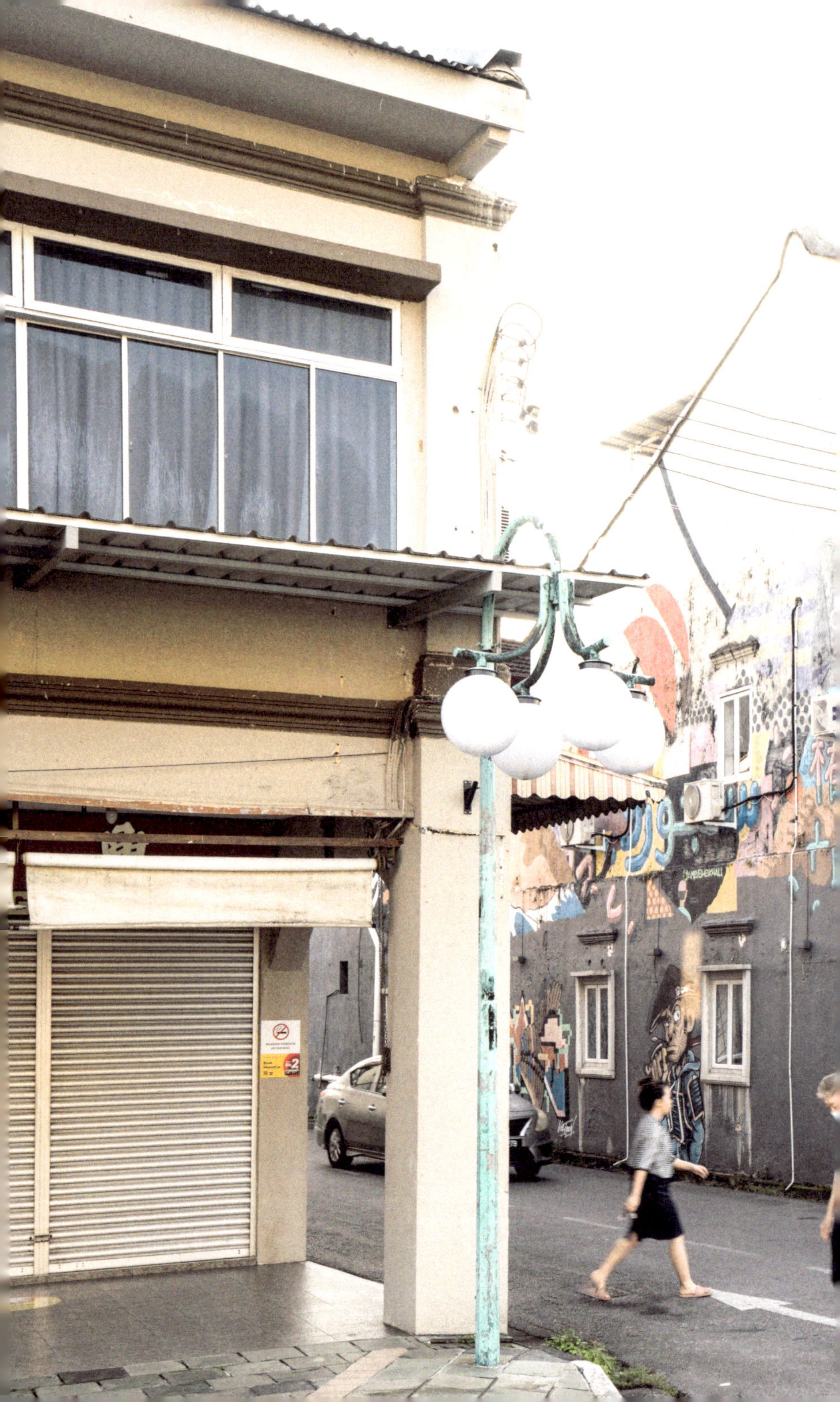

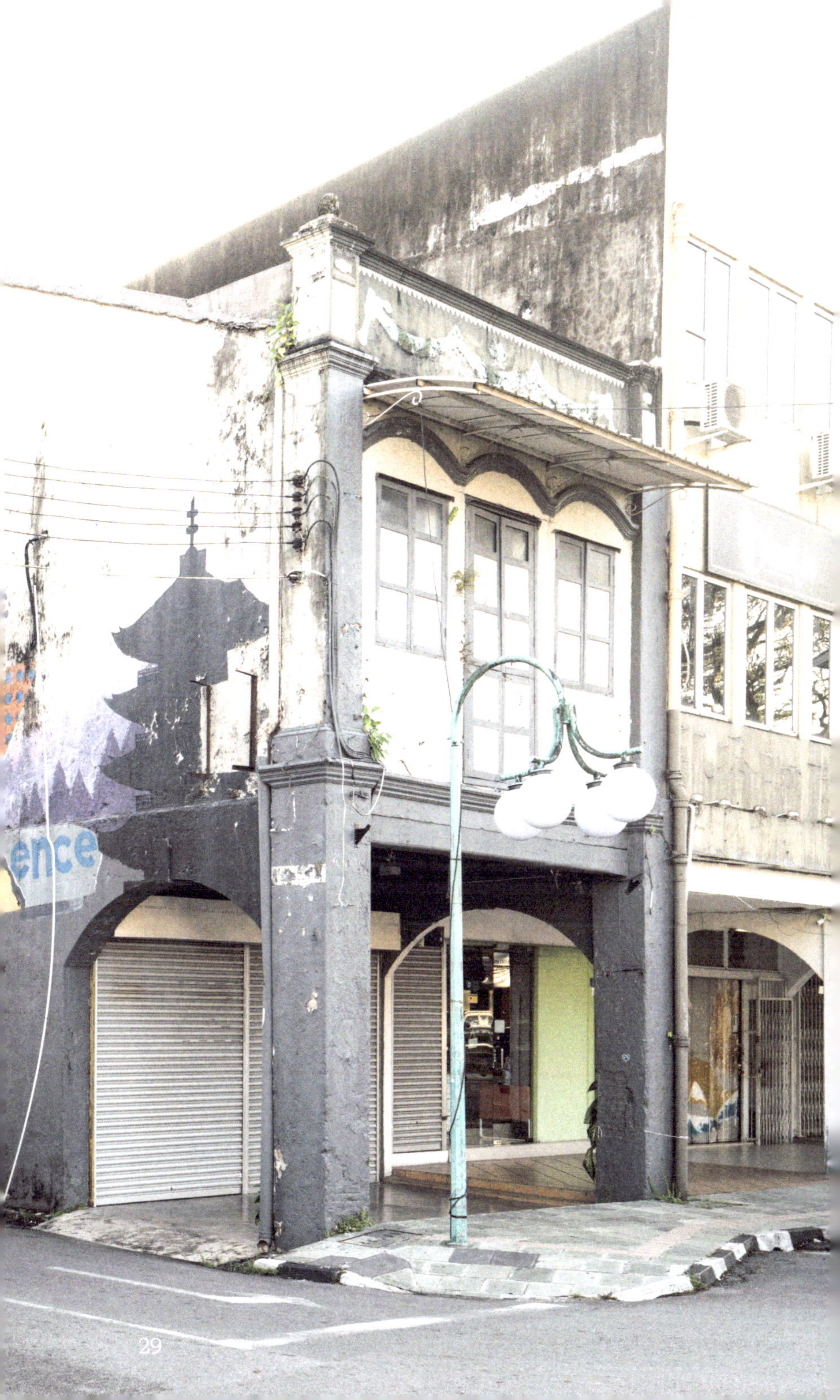
ence

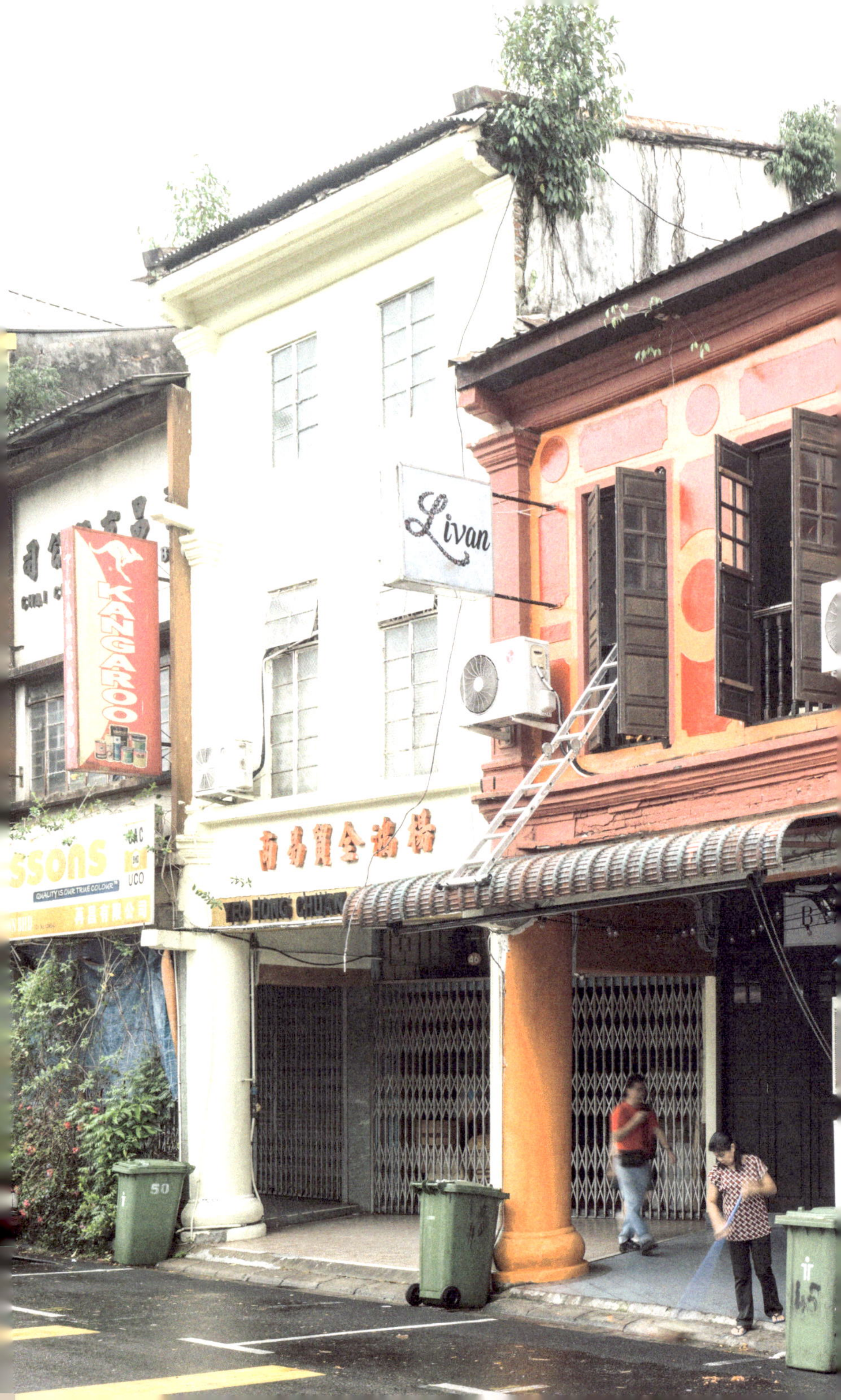
KANGAROO
Livan
ssons
QUALITY IS OUR TRUE COLOUR
UCO
50
45

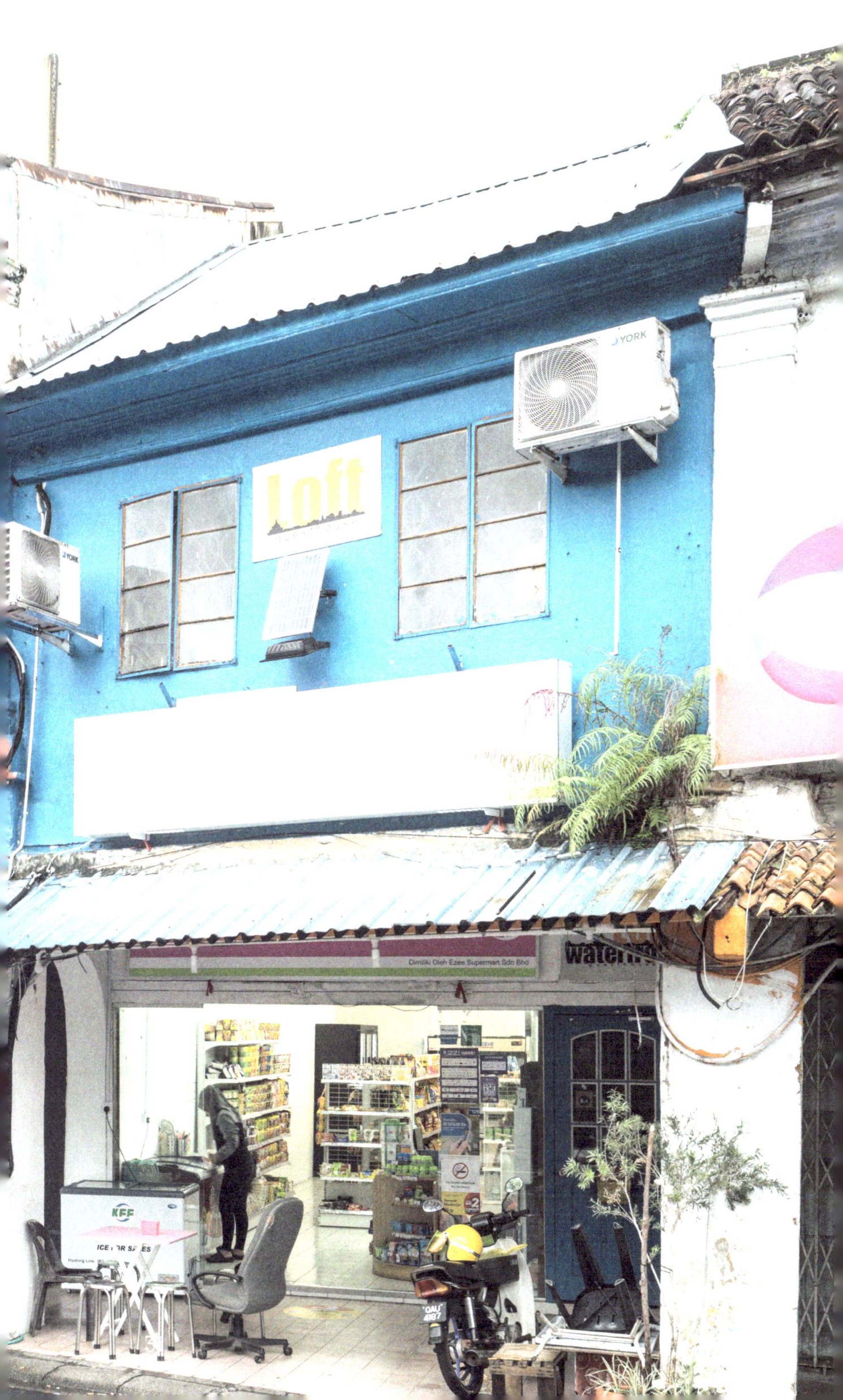
Loft
YORK
Dimiliki Oleh Ezee Supermart Sdn Bhd
KFF

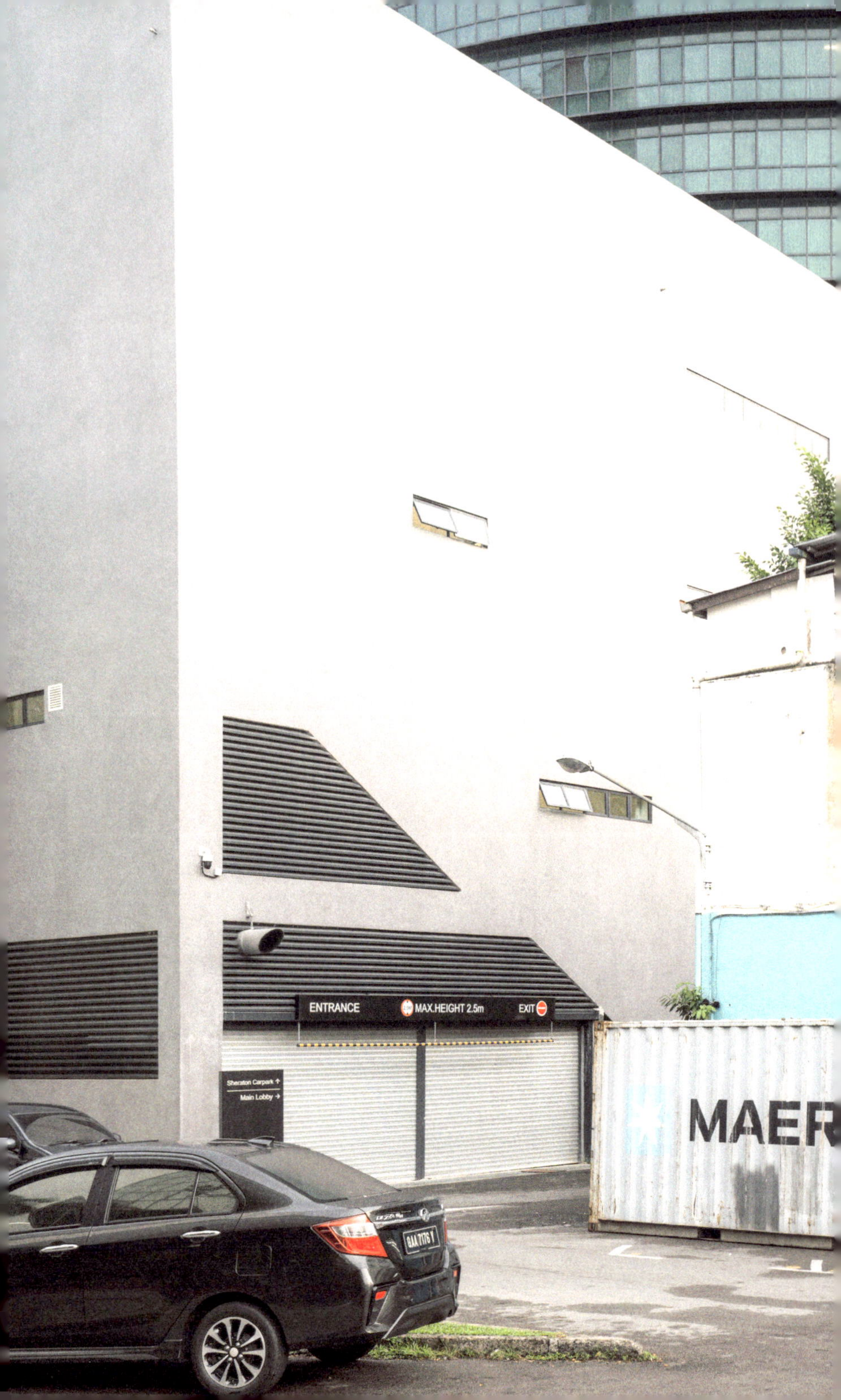
ENTRANCE
MAX.HEIGHT 2.5m
EXIT
Sheraton Carpark
Main Lobby
MAER

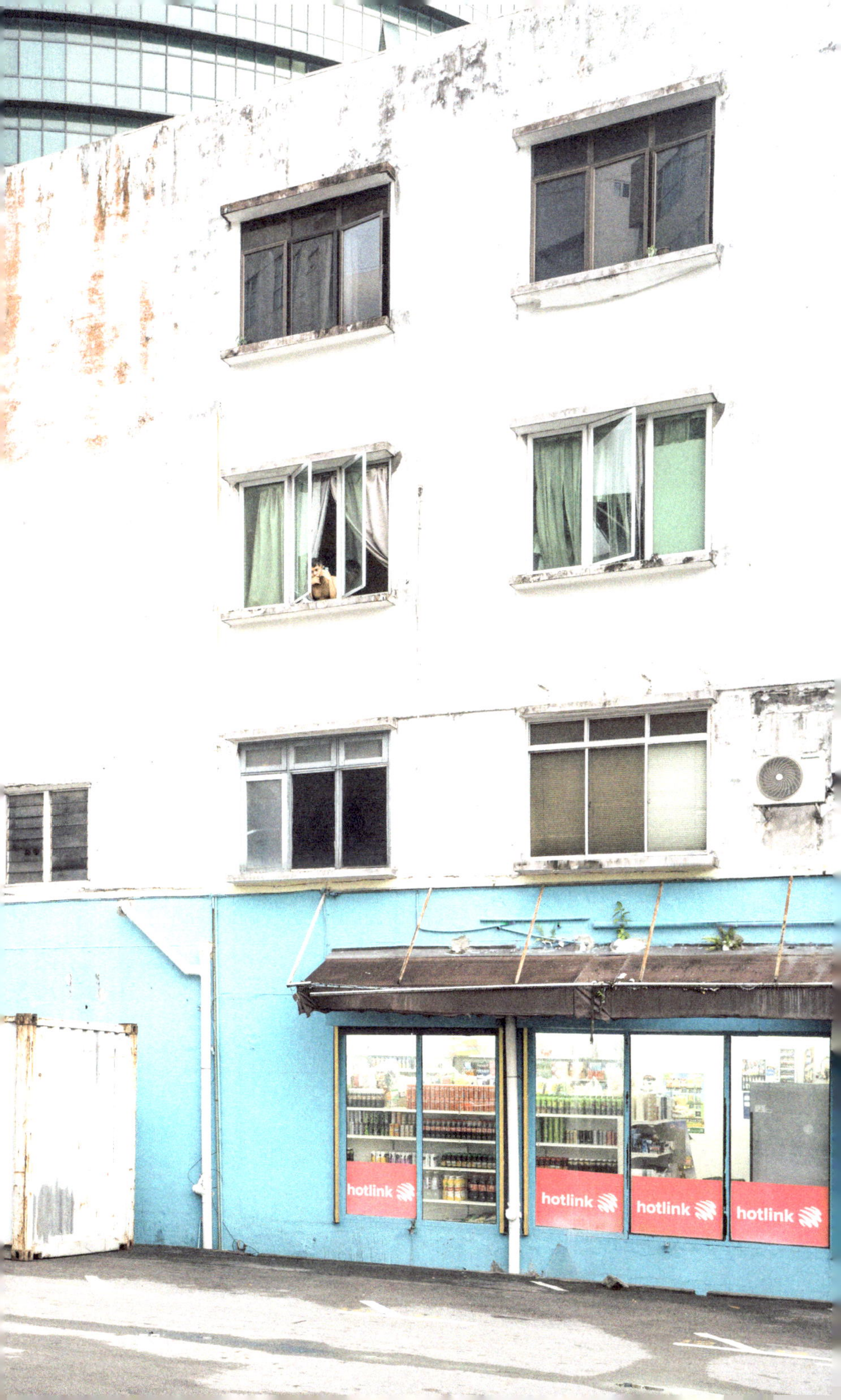
hotlink
hotlink
hotlink
hotlink

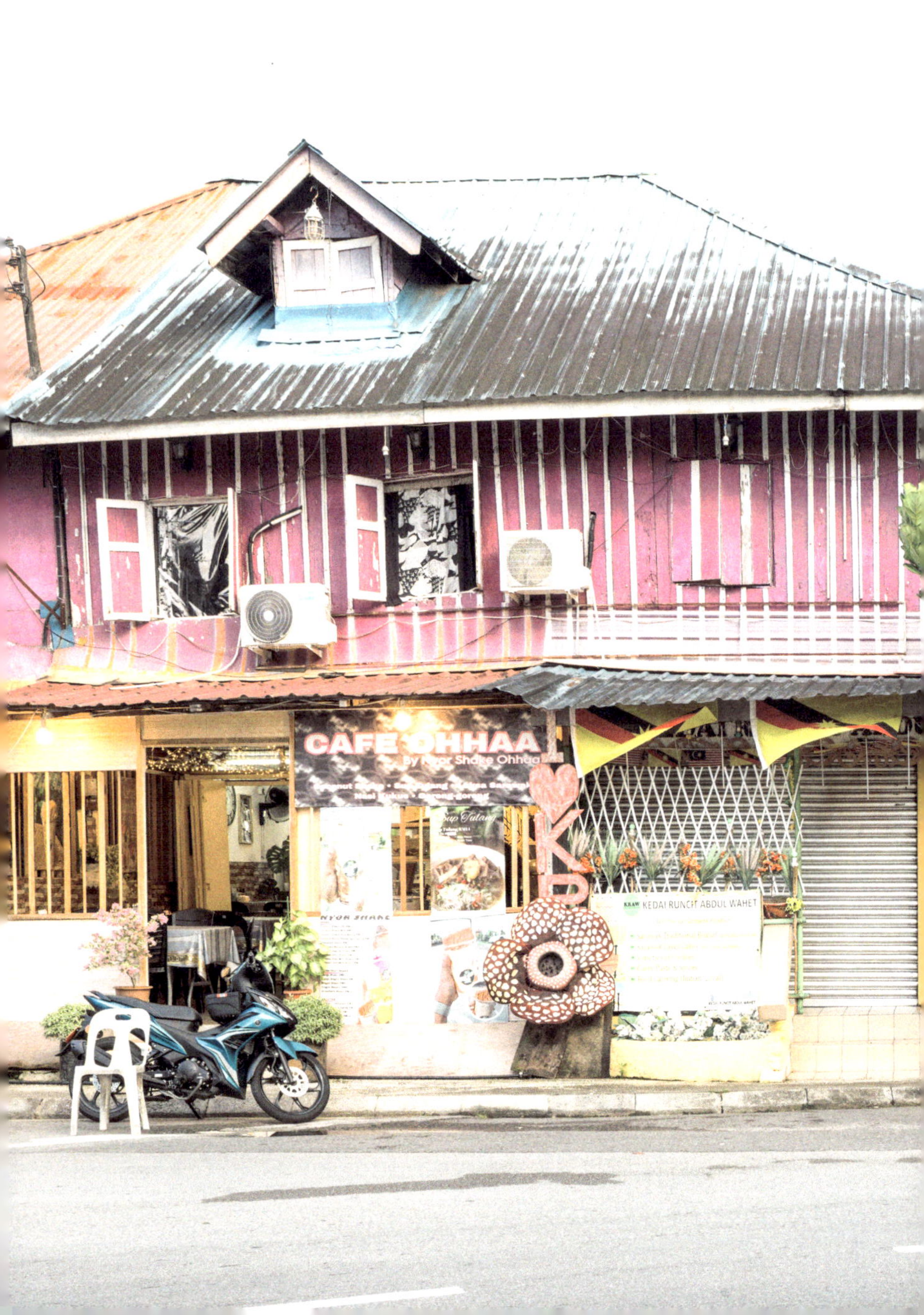
CAFE OHHAA
KEDAI RUNCIT ABDUL WAHET

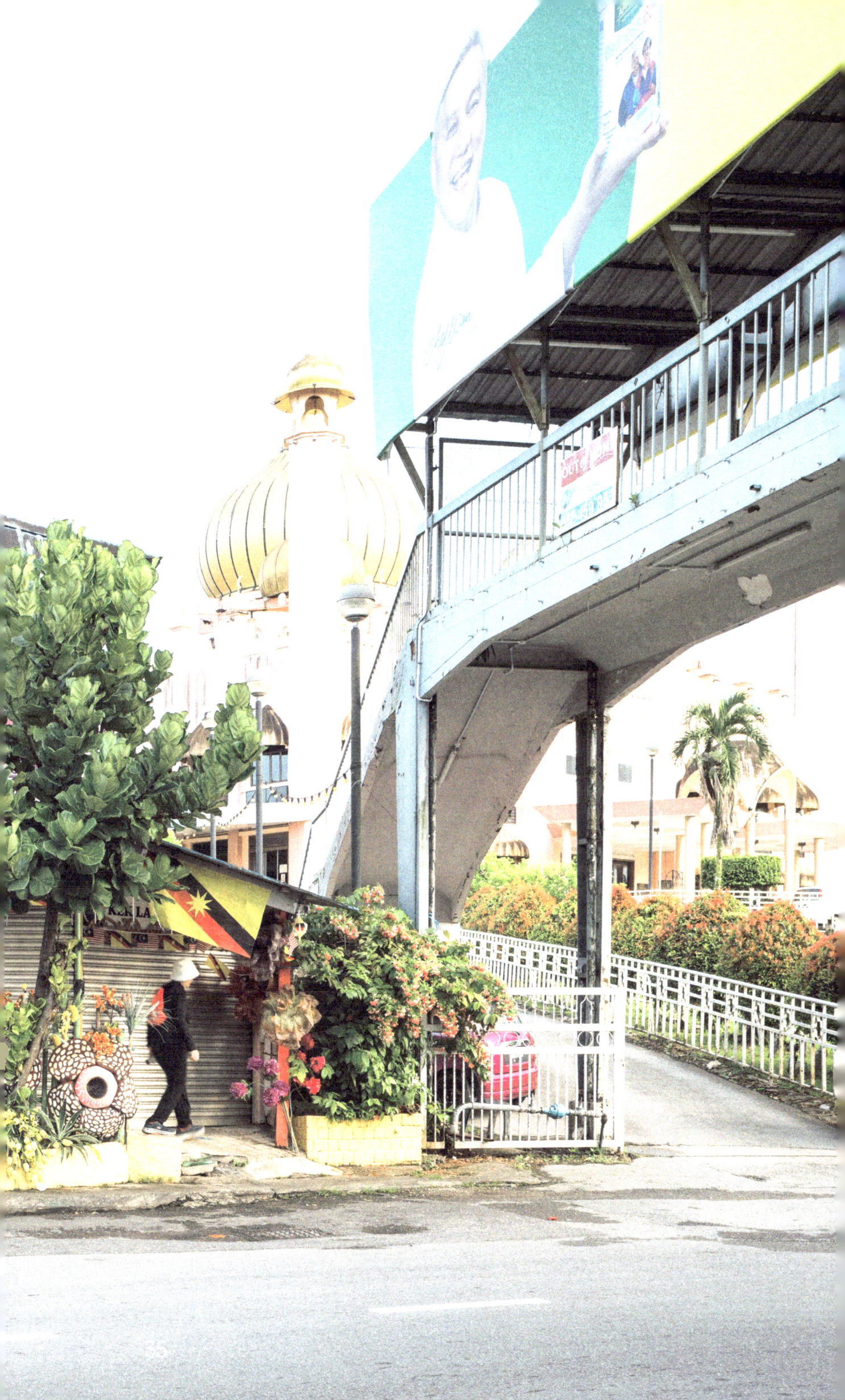

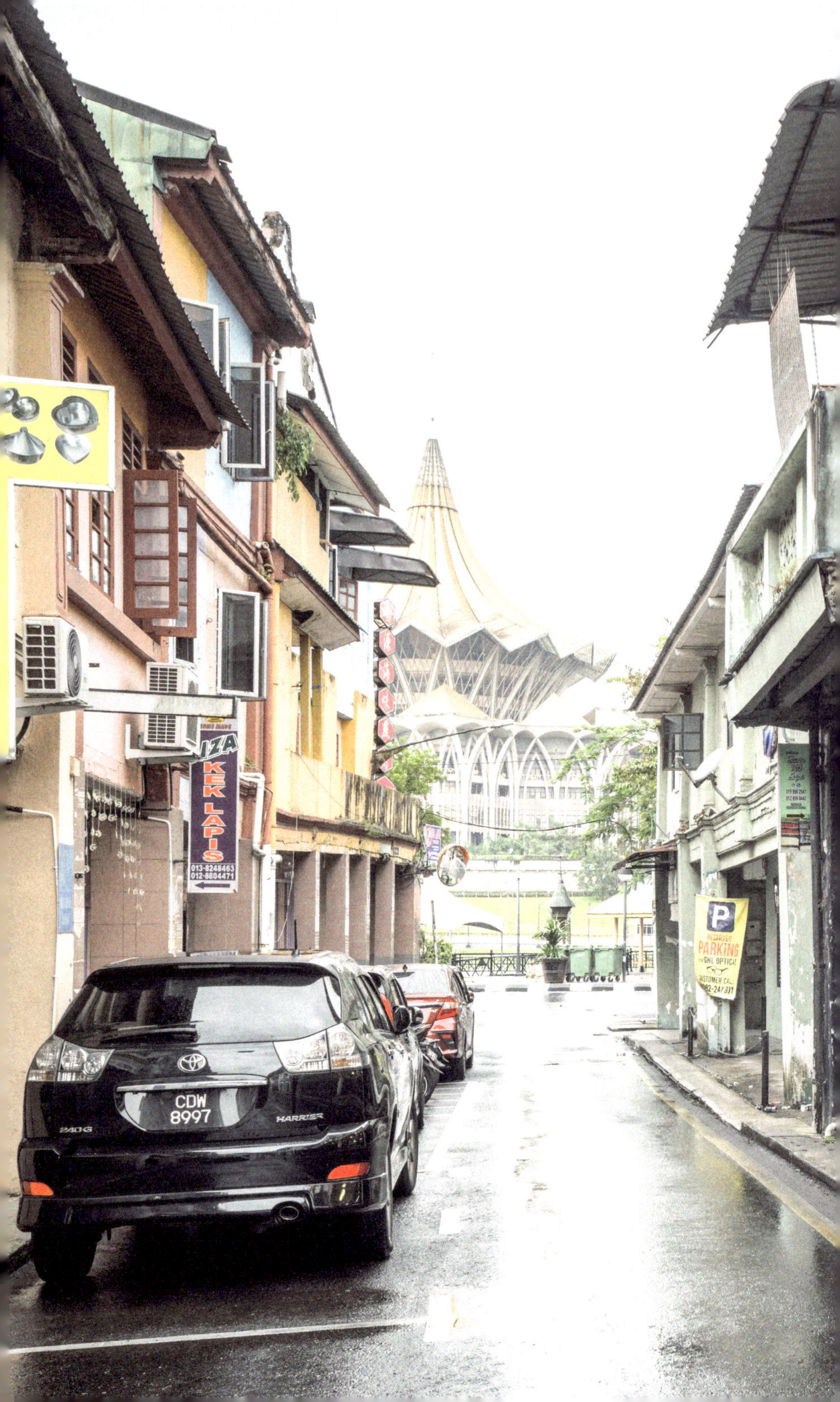
KEK LAPIS
013-8248463
012-8804471
CDW
8997
HARRIER
240G
P
RESERVED
PARKING

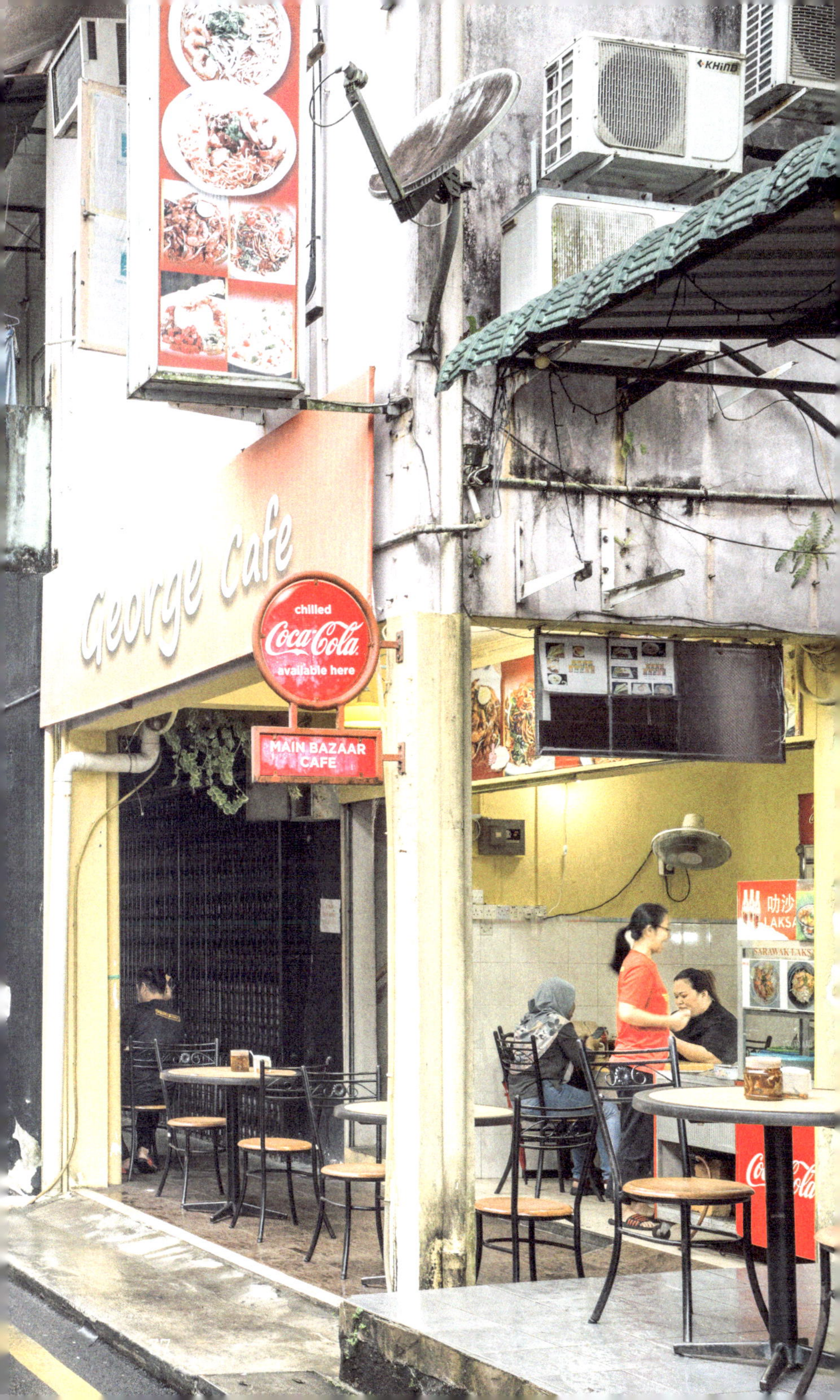
KHIND
George Cafe
chilled
Coca-Cola
available here
MAIN BAZAAR
CAFE
叻沙
LAKSA
SARAWAK LAKSA
Coca-Cola

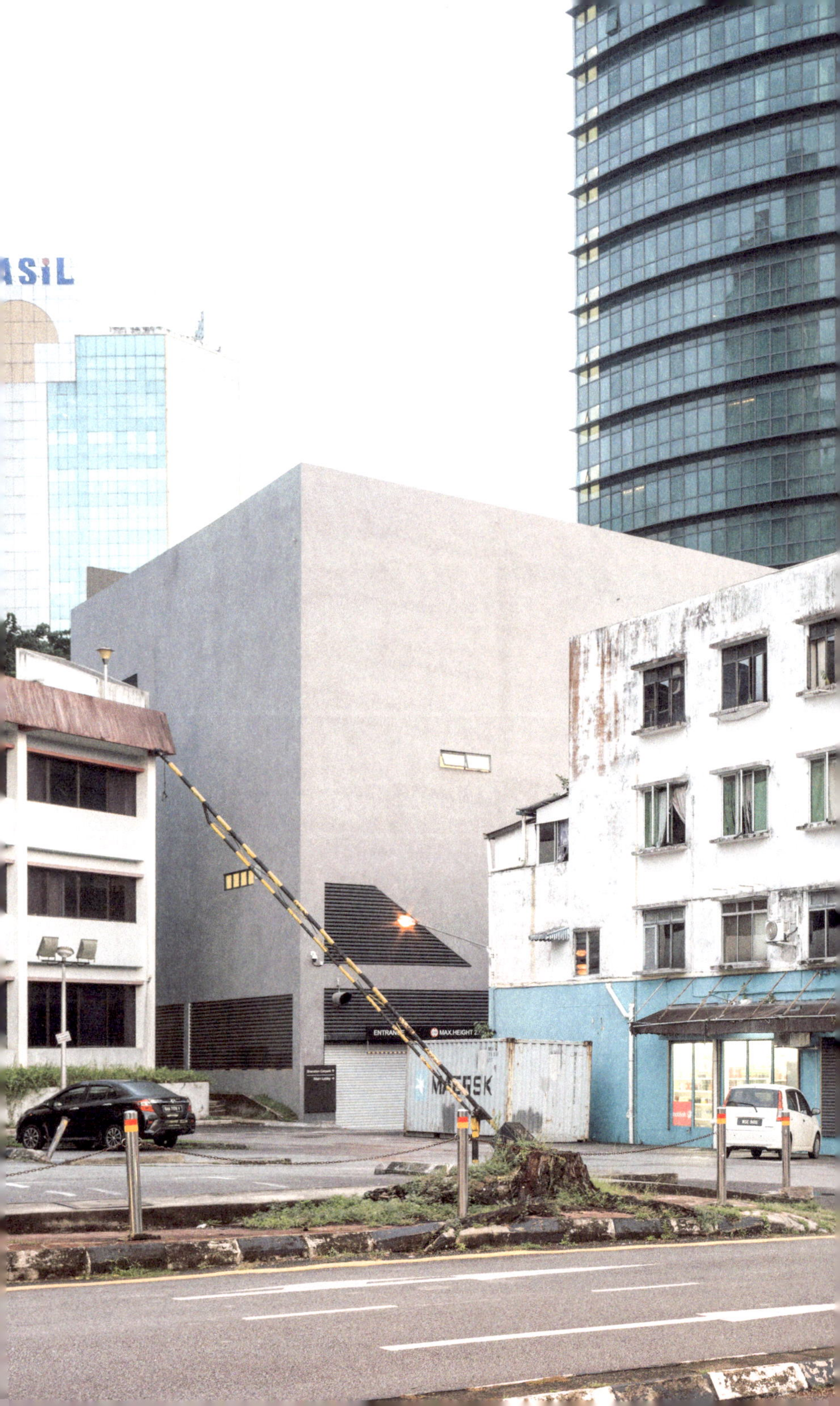
ASIL
MAX.HEIGHT

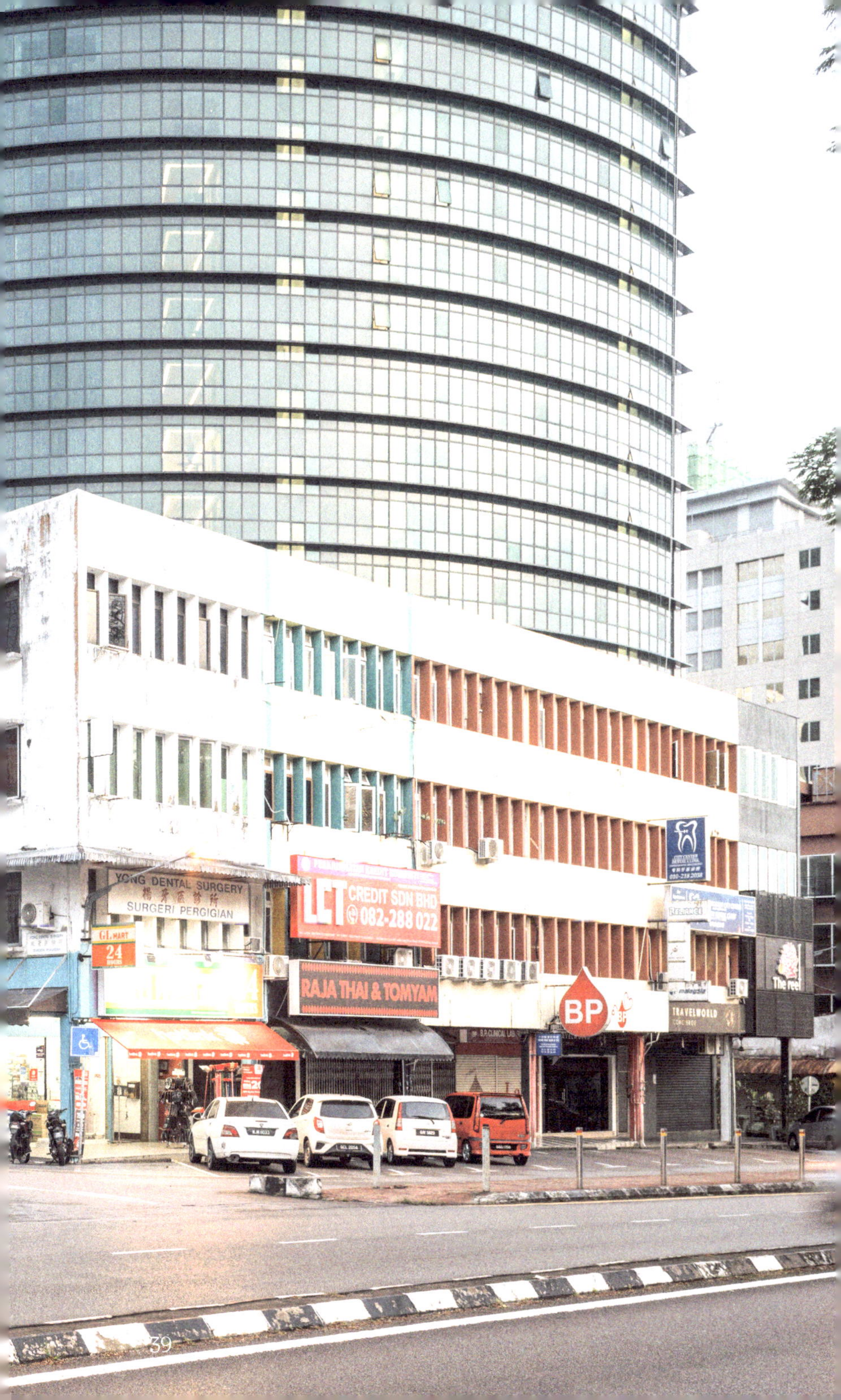
YONG DENTAL SURGERY
SURGERI PERGIGIAN
GL MART
24
LCT CREDIT SDN BHD
082-288 022
RAJA THAI & TOMYAM
BP
TRAVELWORLD
The reef

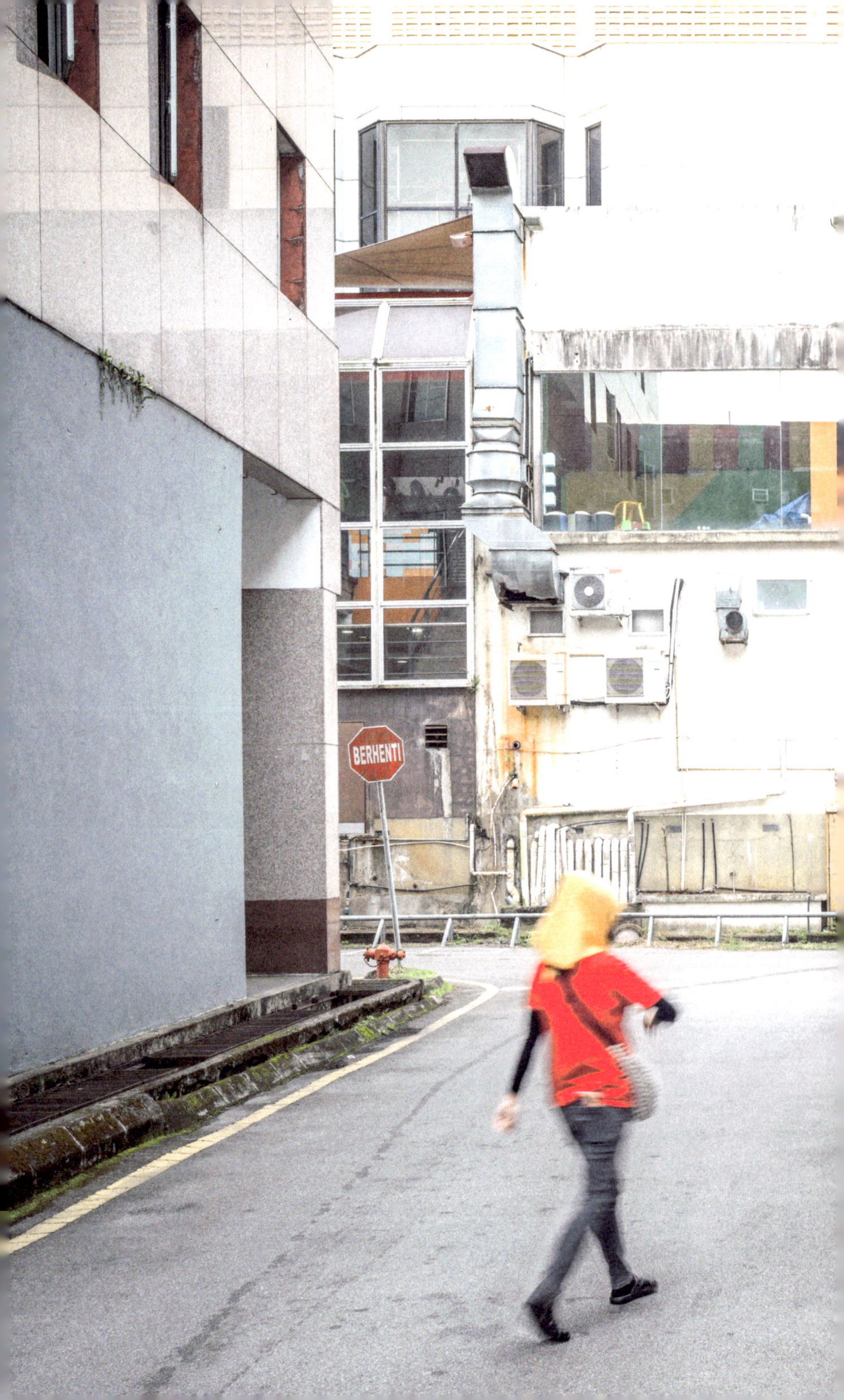
BERHENTI

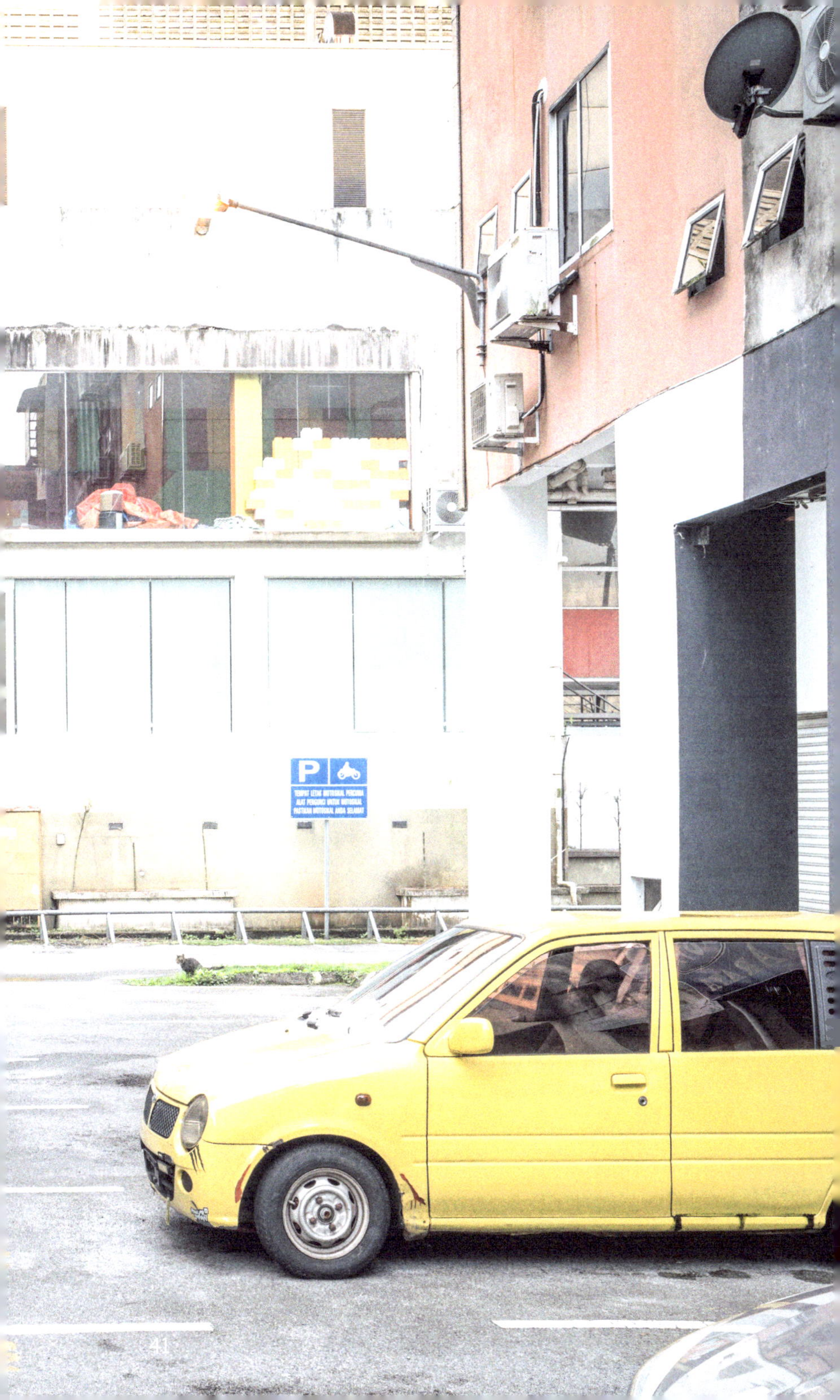
P
TEMPAT LETAK MOTOSIKAL PERCUMA
ALAT PENGUNCI UNTUK MOTOSIKAL
PASTIKAN MOTOSIKAL ANDA SELAMAT

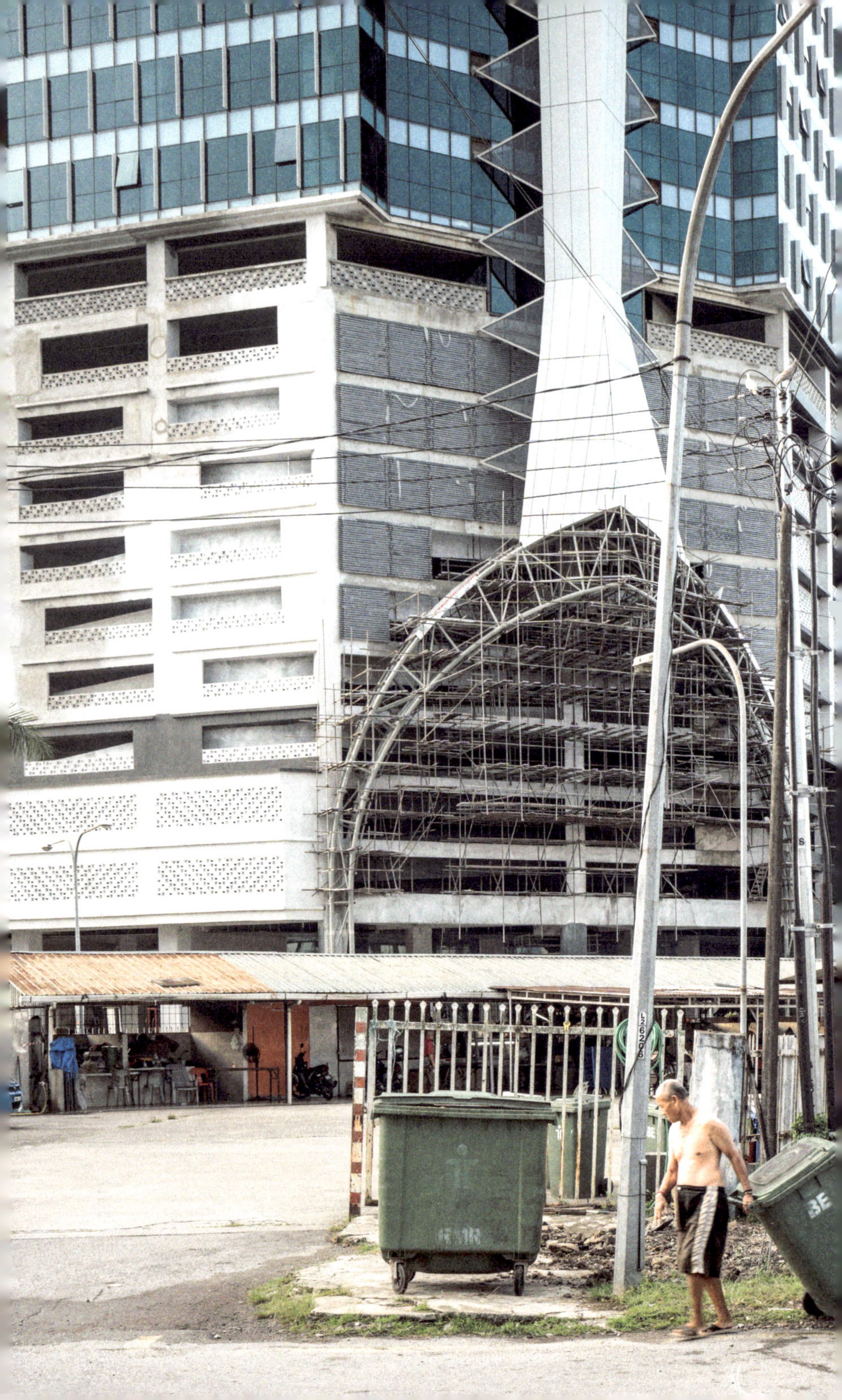
L26206
BE

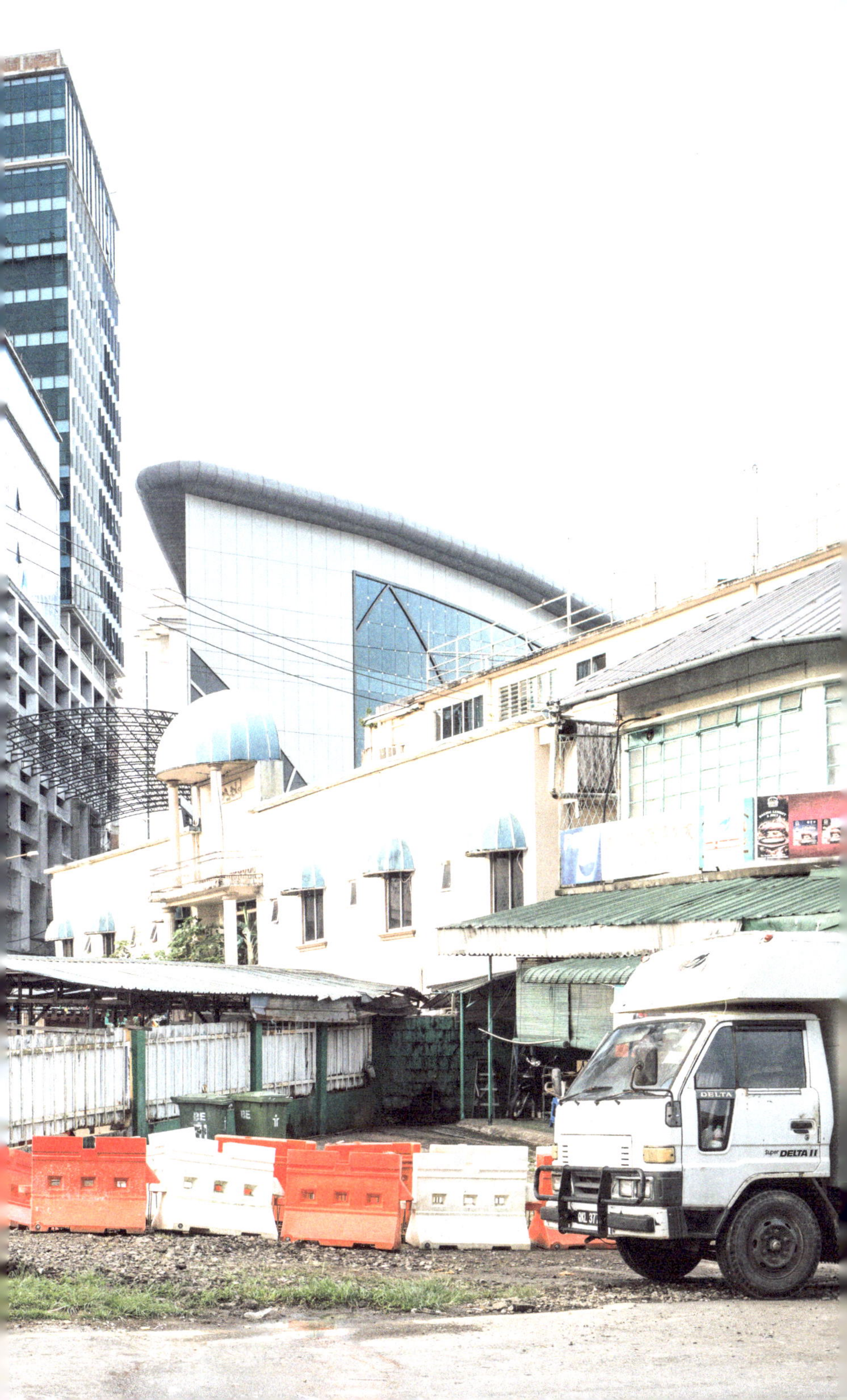
DELTA
super DELTA II

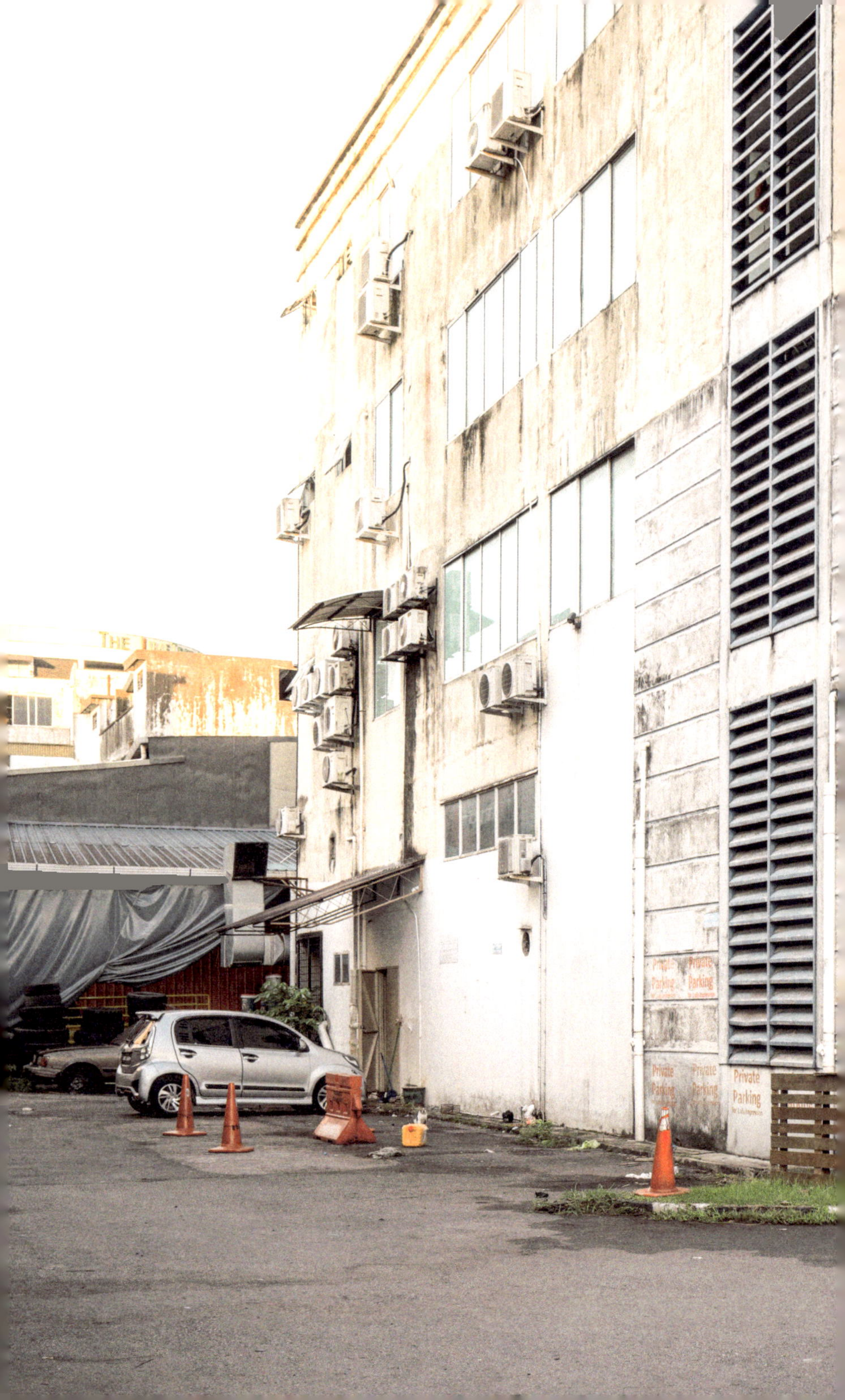
THE
Private Parking
Private Parking
Private Parking
Private Parking
Private Parking

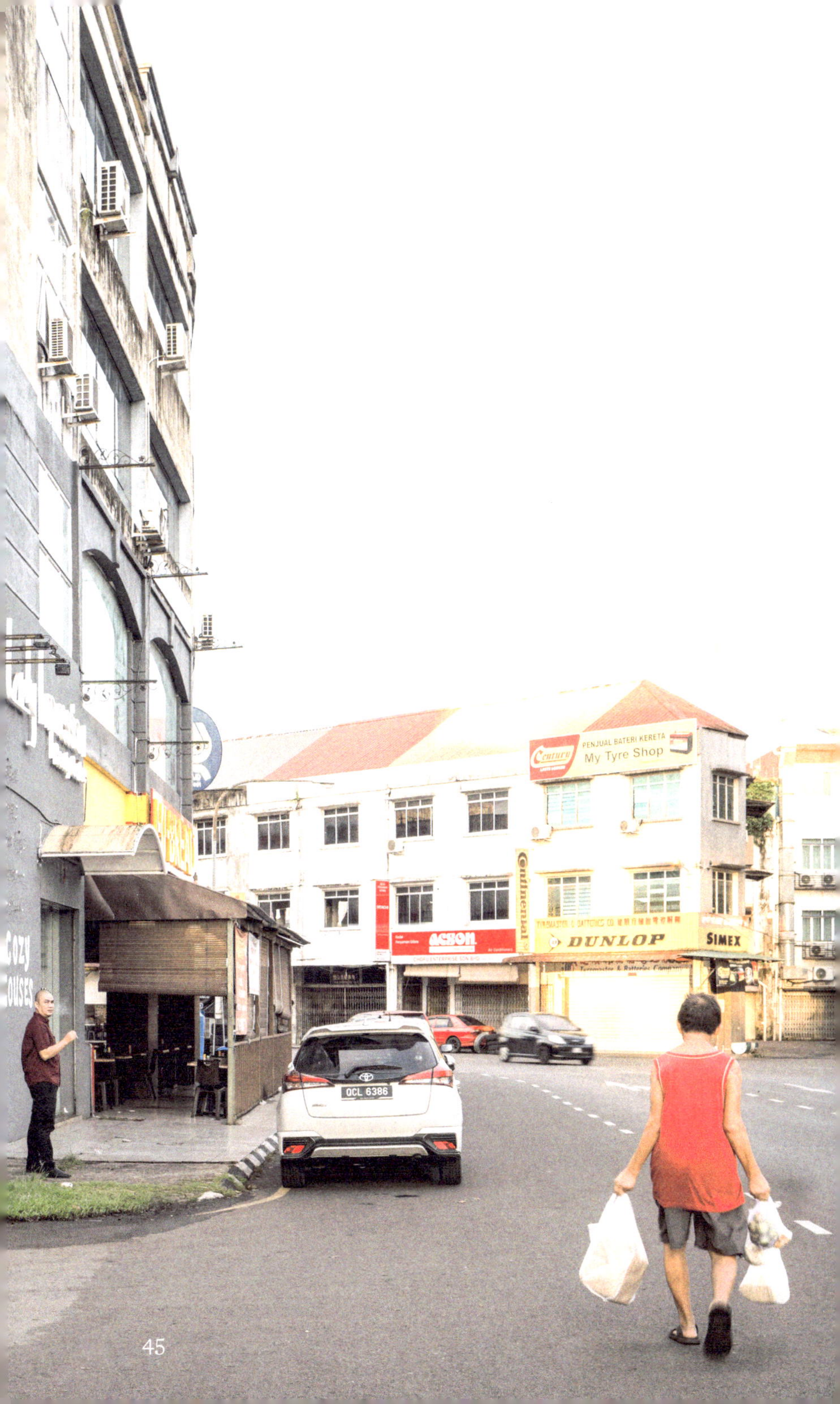
PENJUAL BATERI KERETA
My Tyre Shop
Century
DUNLOP
SIMEX
ACSON
QCL 6386
Cozy

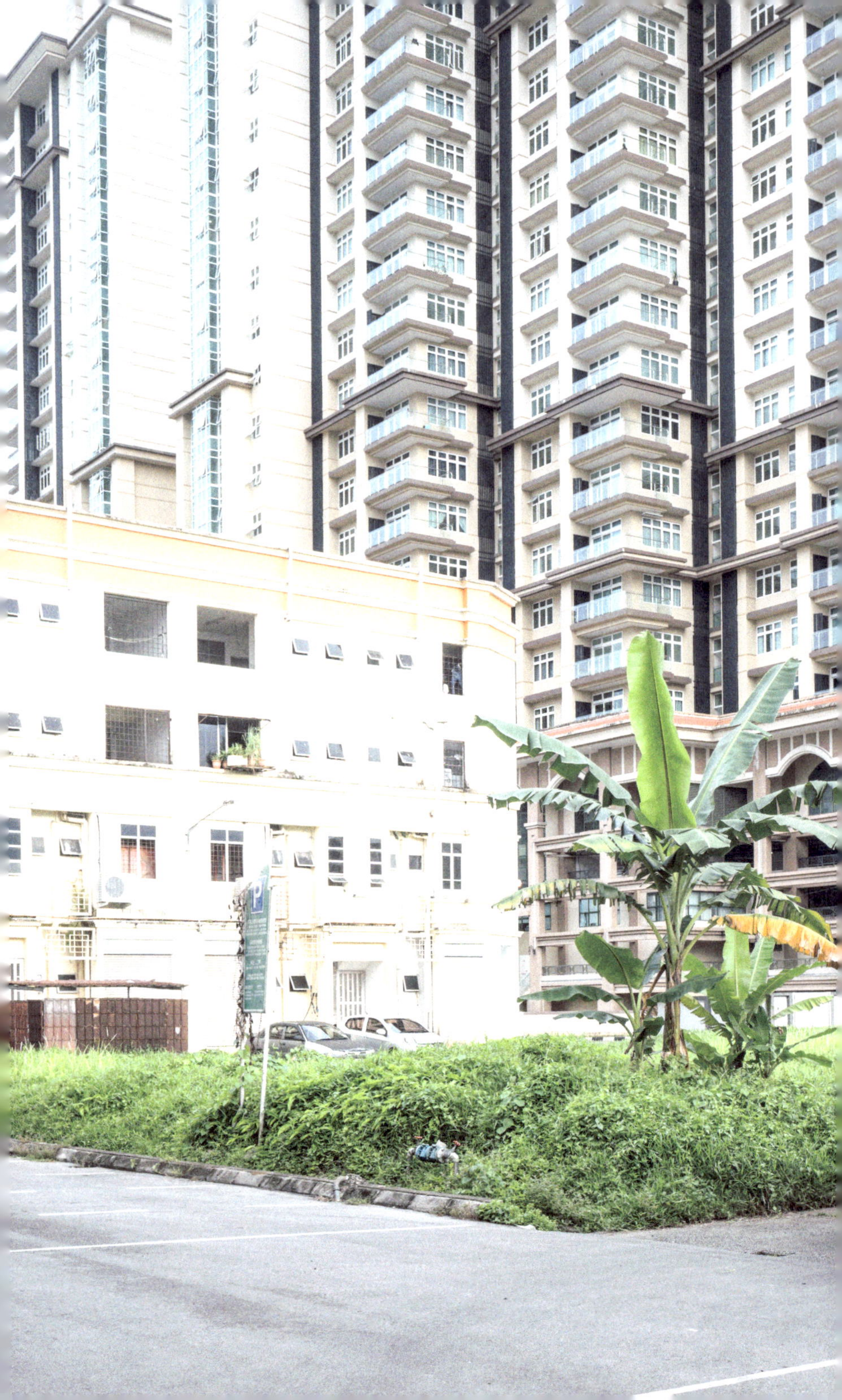
P

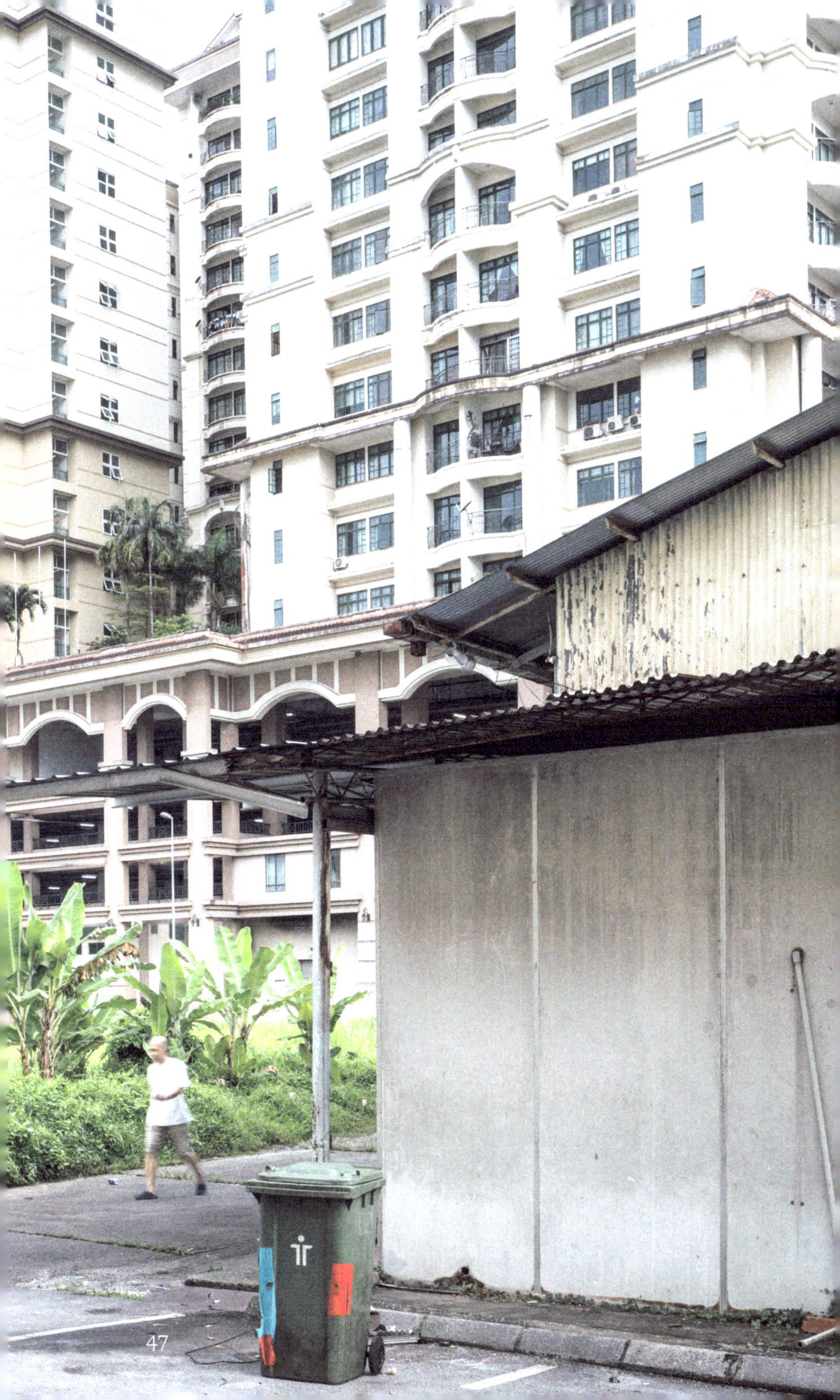

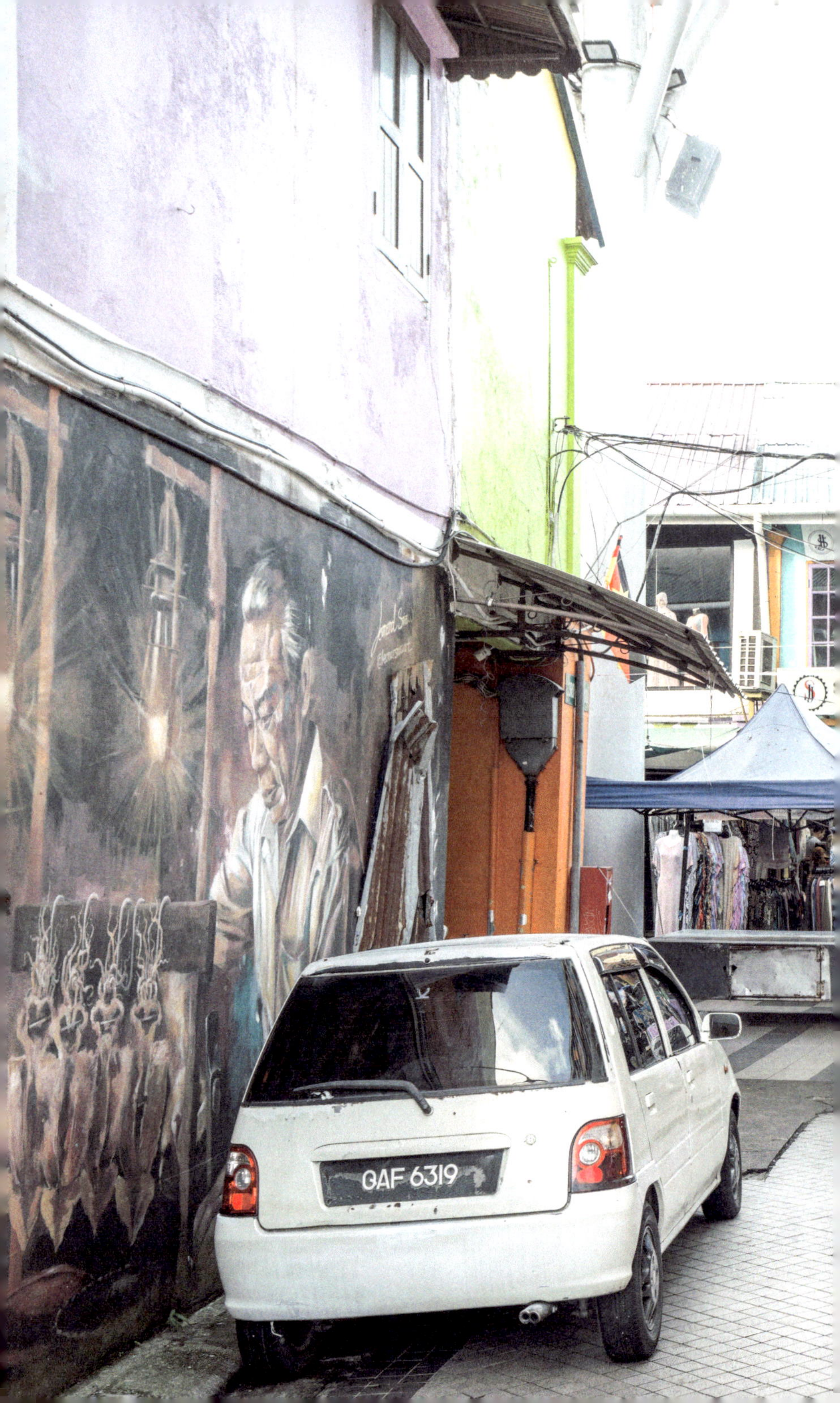
QAF 6319

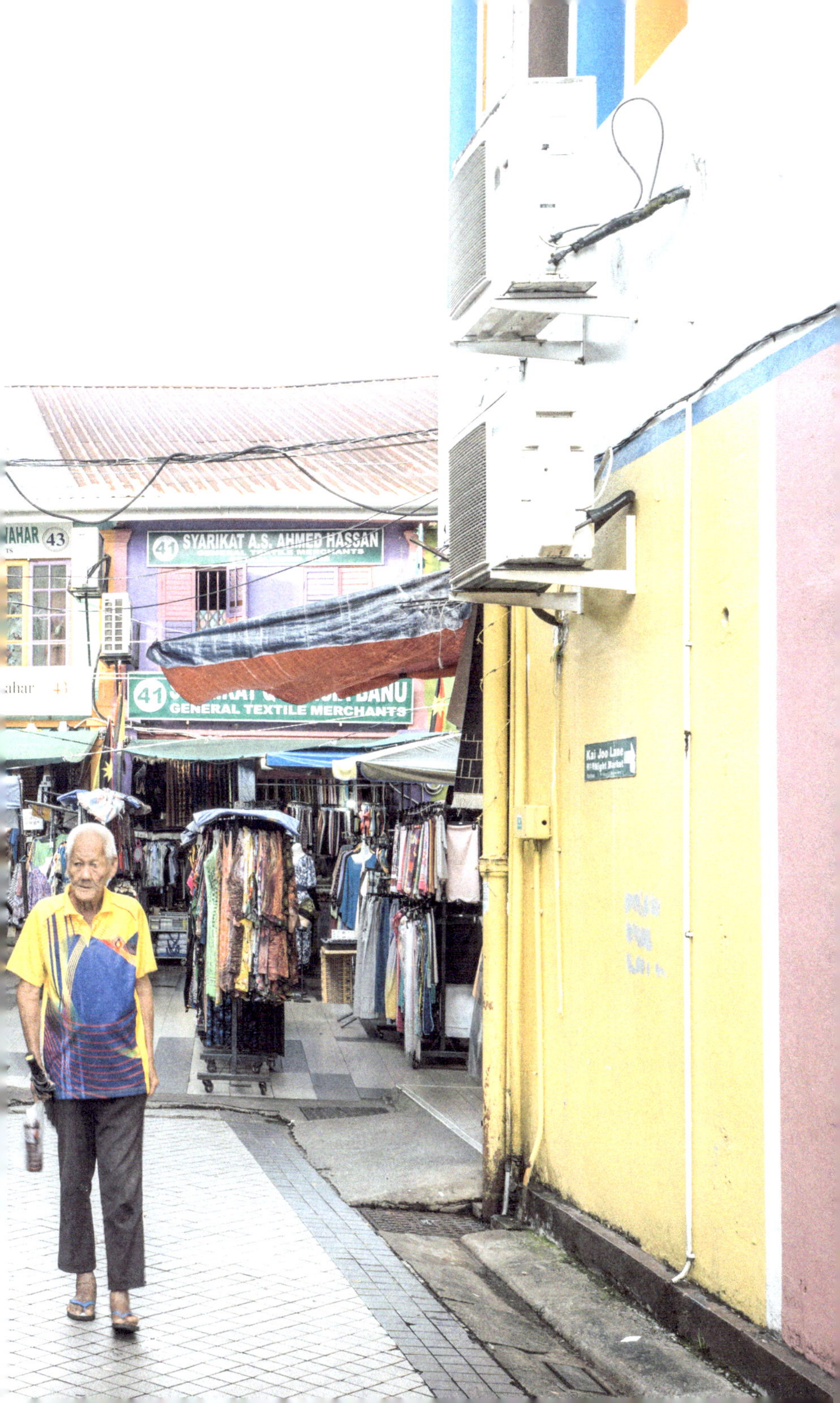

43
41
SYARIKAT A.S. AHMED HASSAN
41
GENERAL TEXTILE MERCHANTS
Kai Joo Lane

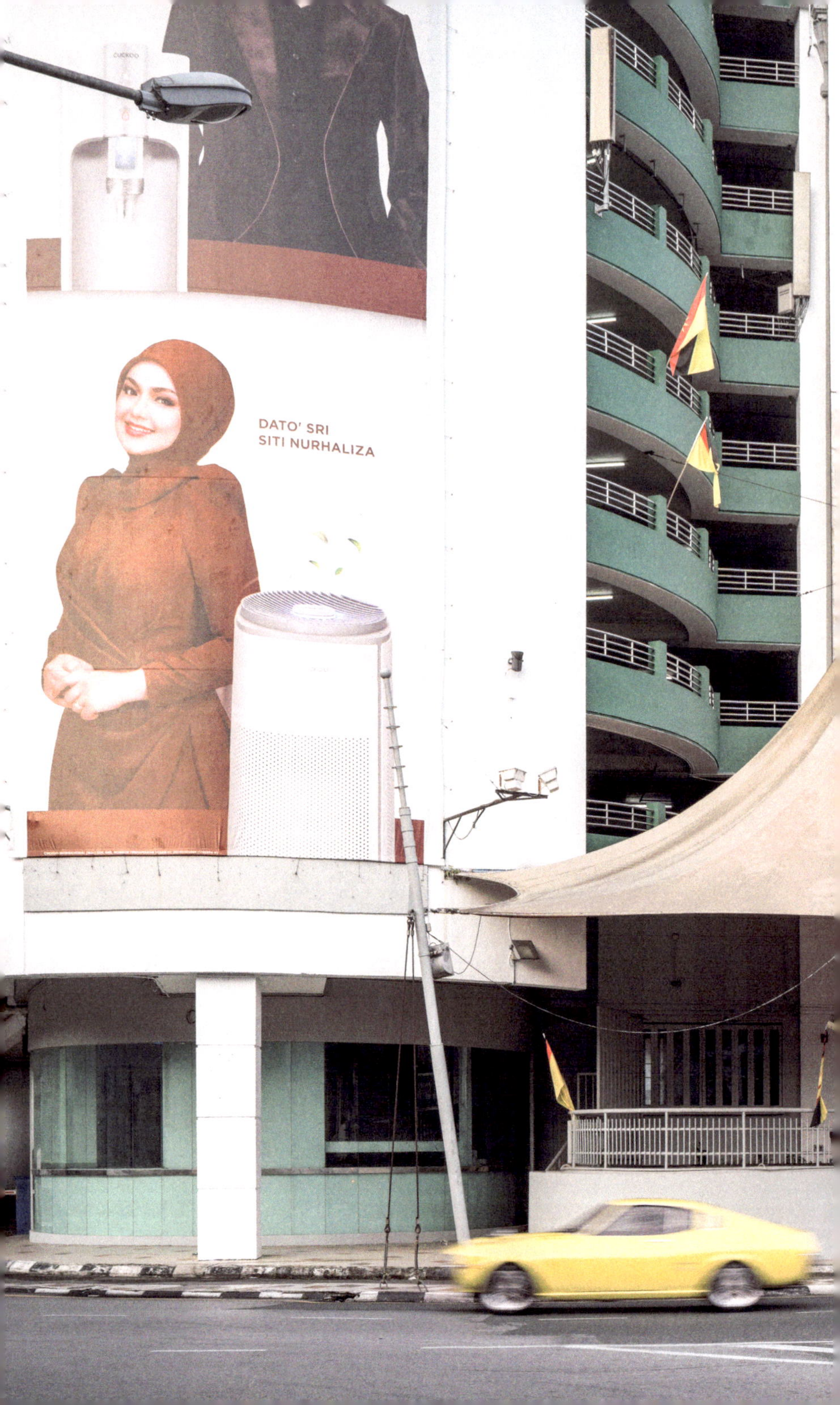
DATO' SRI
SITI NURHALIZA

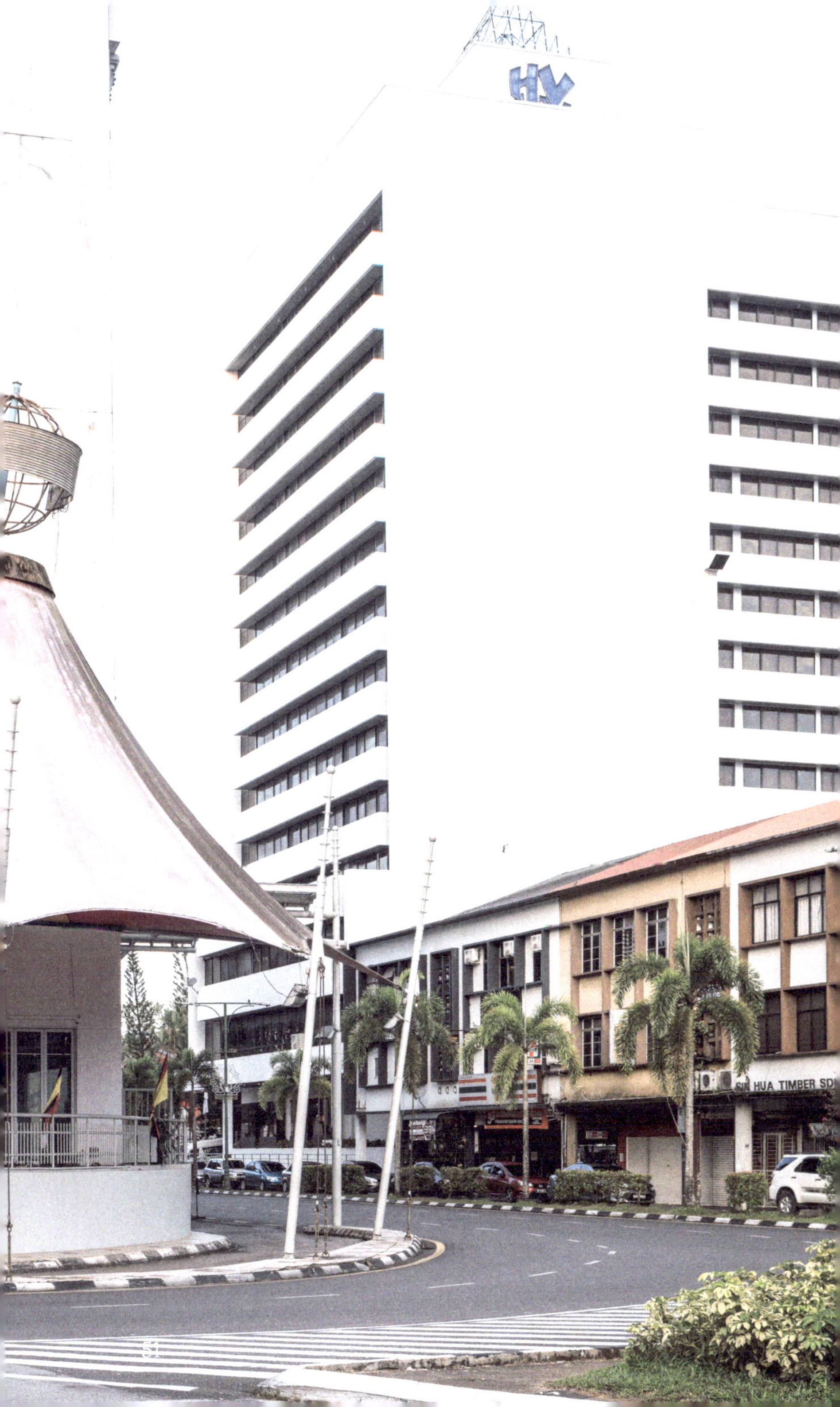
HV
HUA TIMBER

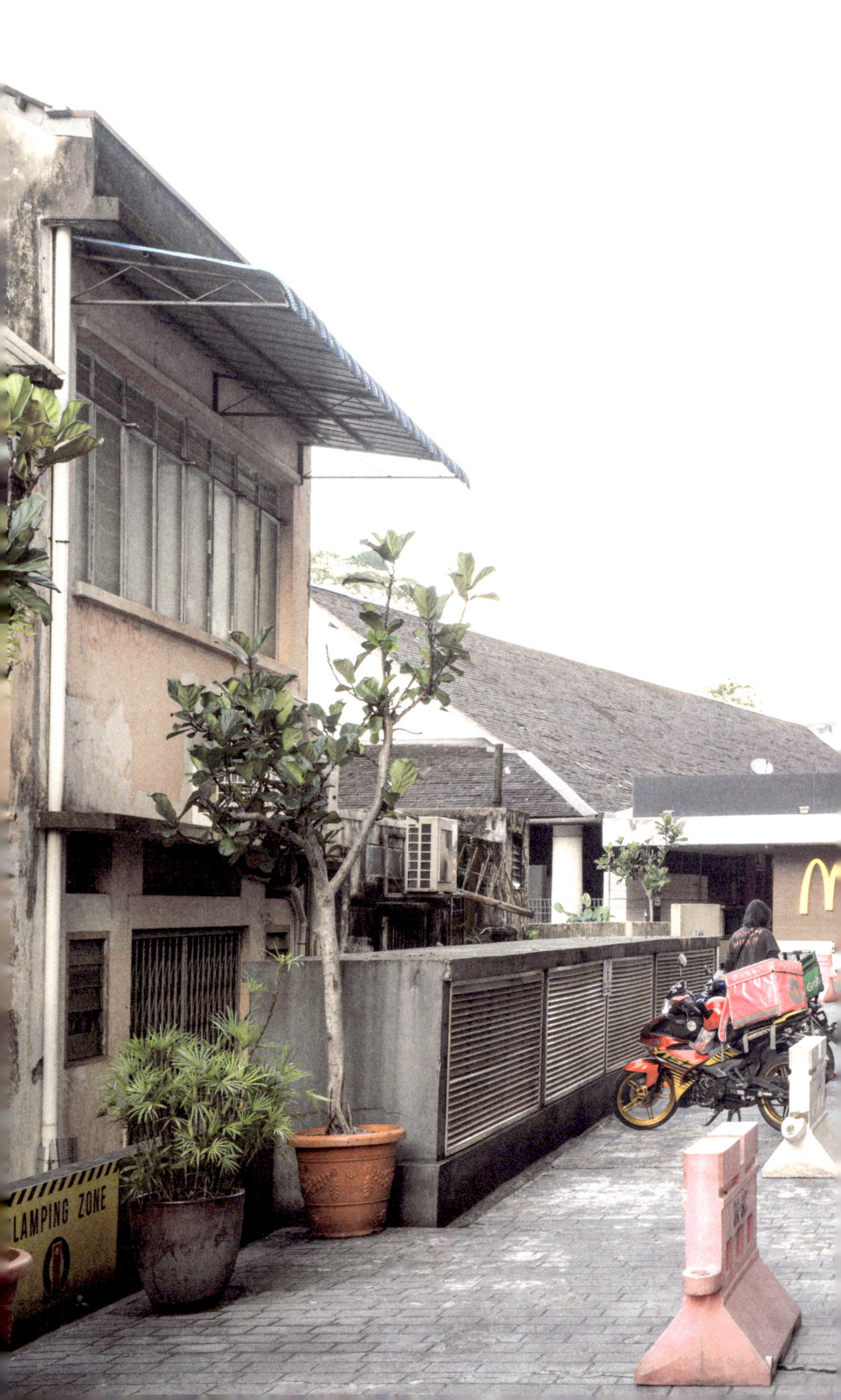
LAMPING ZONE

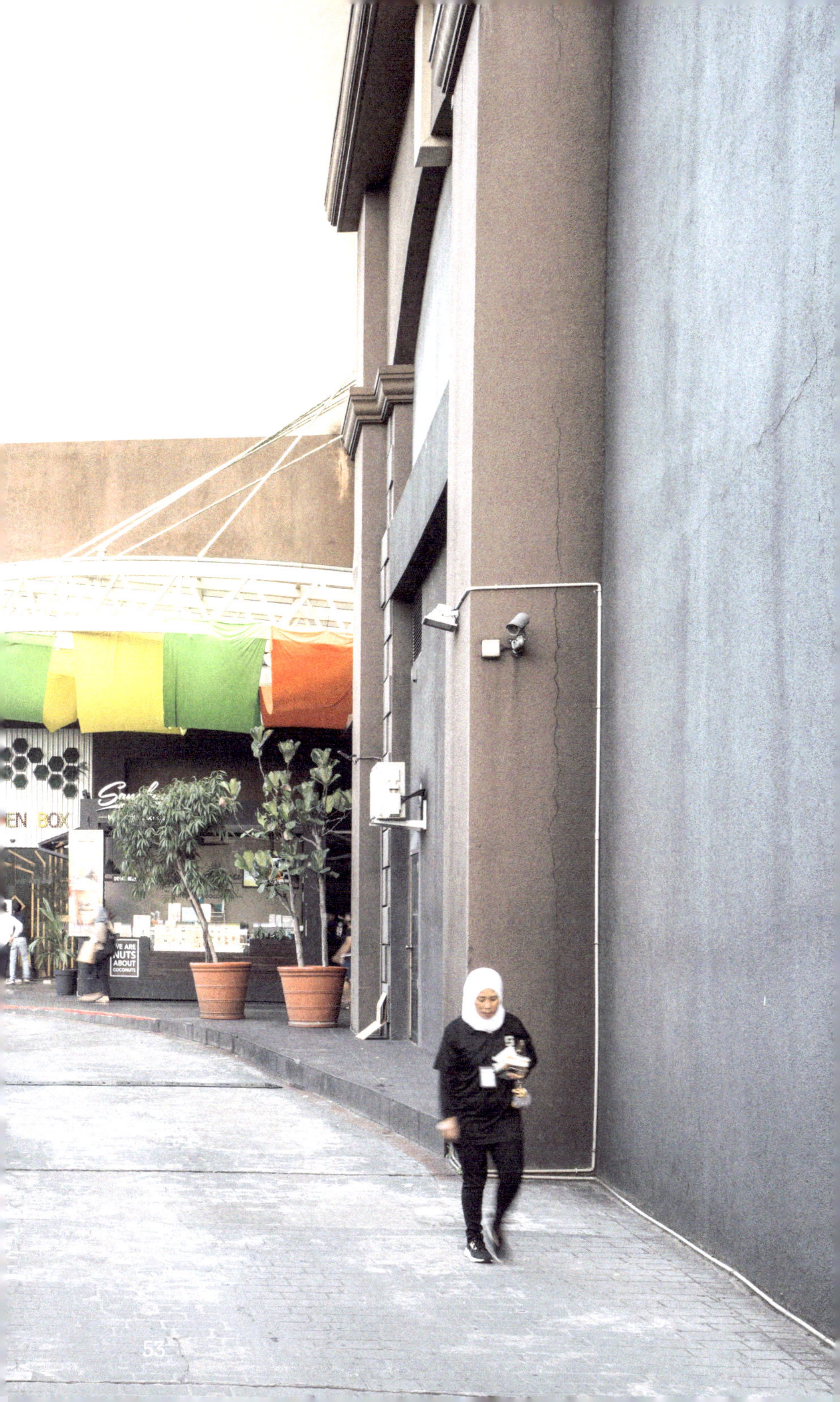
EN BOX
VE ARE
NUTS
ABOUT
COCONUTS

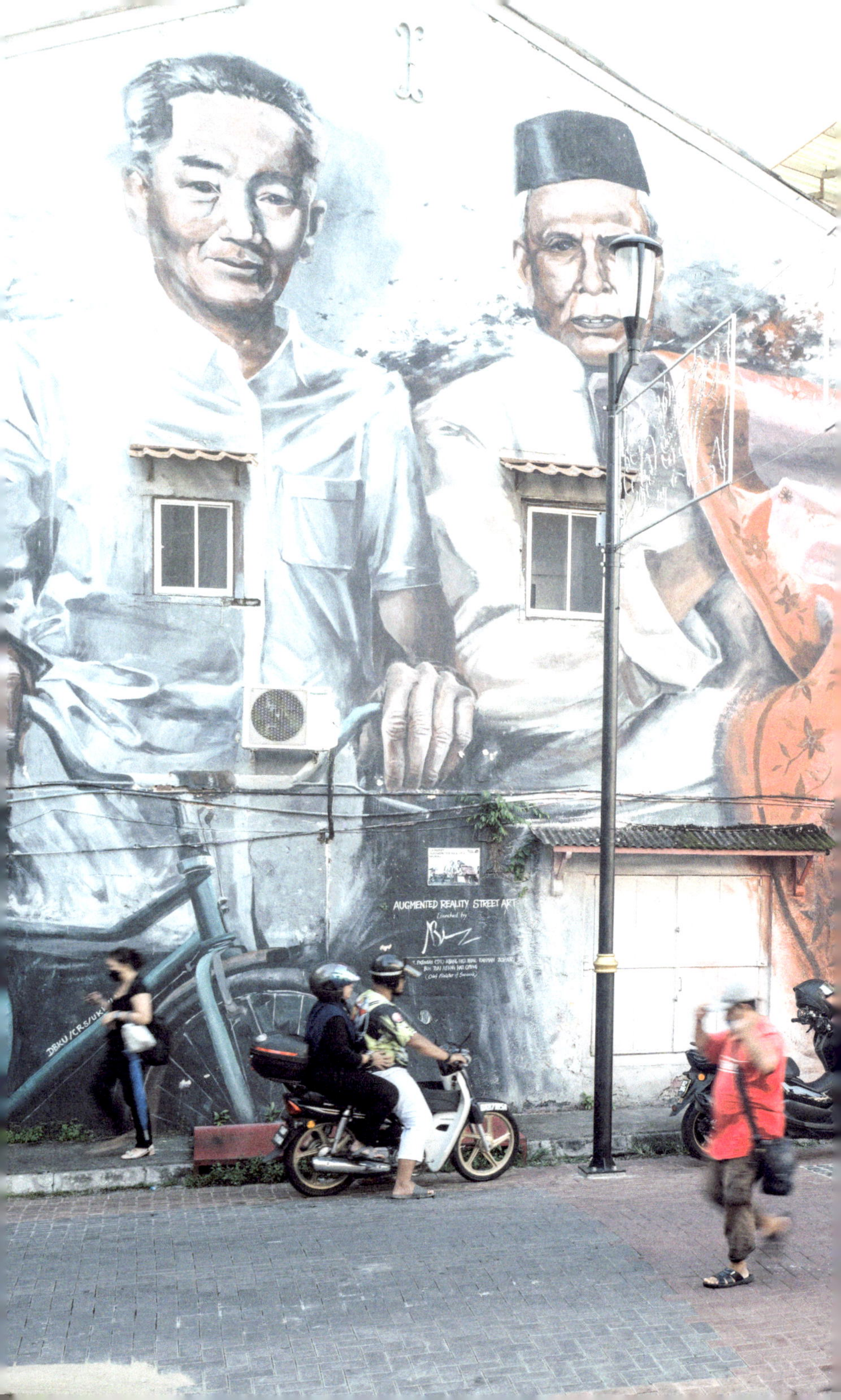
AUGMENTED REALITY STREET ART
Launched by

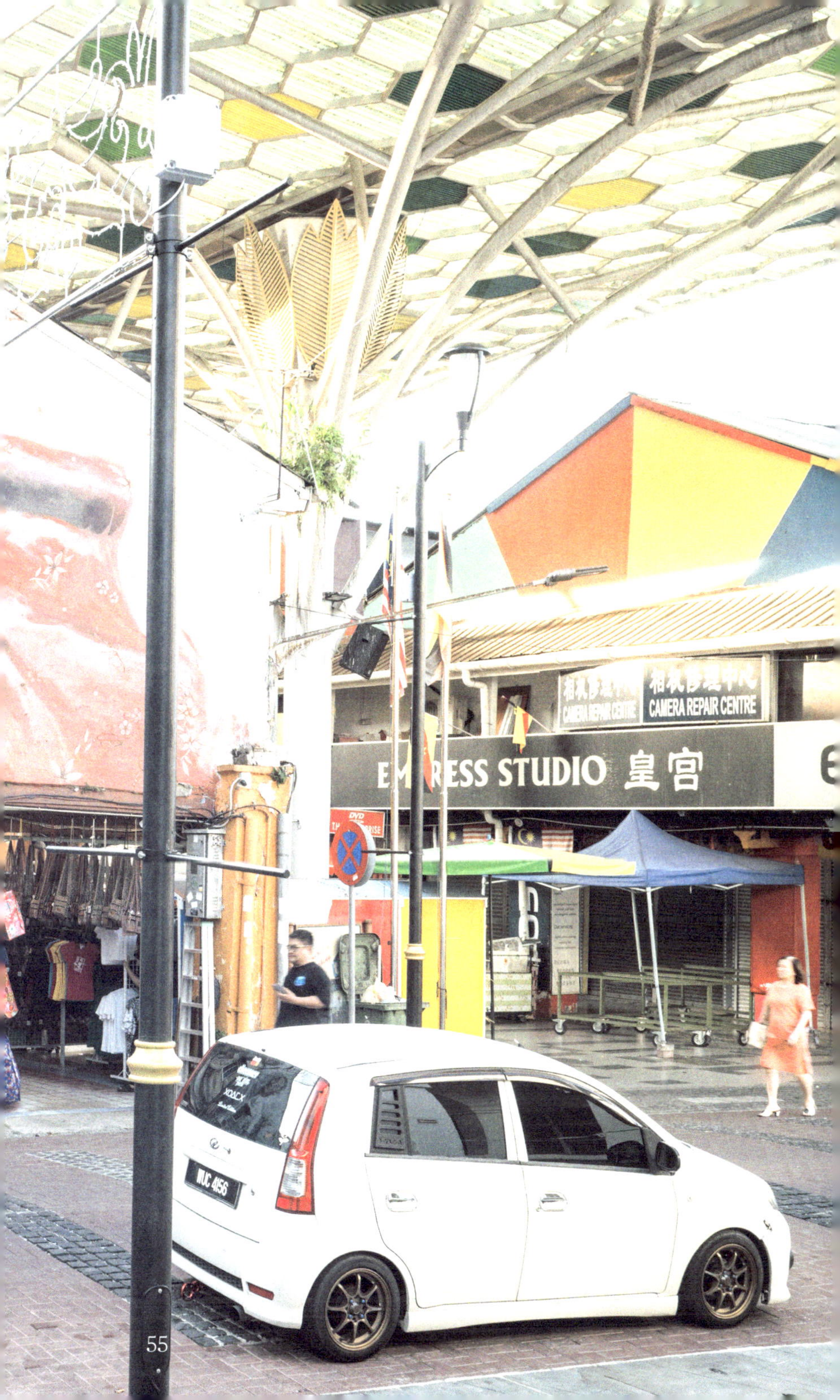
CAMERA REPAIR CENTRE
STUDIO 皇宫
WUC 4156

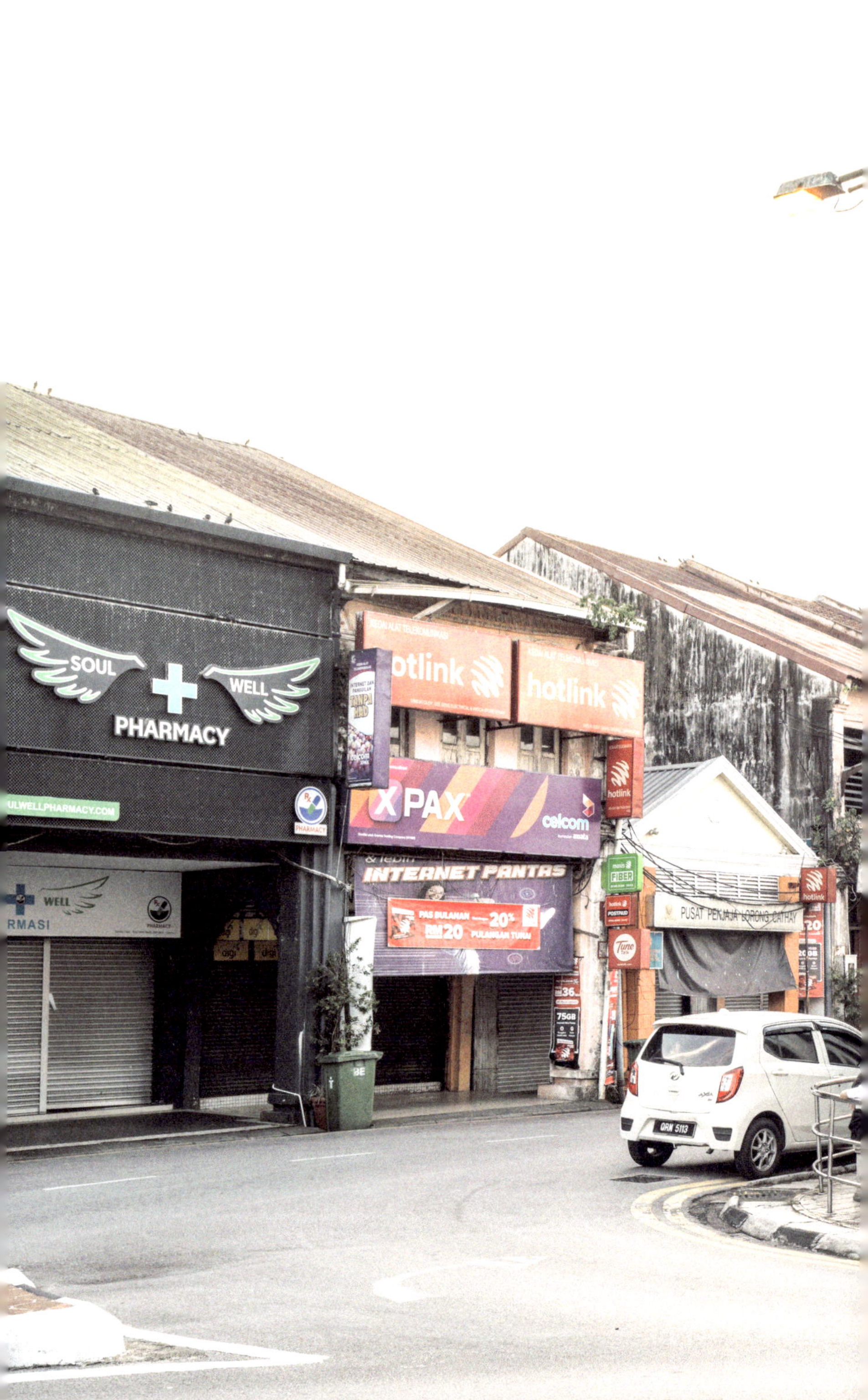
SOUL
WELL
PHARMACY
ULWELLPHARMACY.COM
PHARMACY
WELL
RMASI
otlink
hotlink
TANPA HAD
XPAX
celcom
INTERNET PANTAS
PAS BULANAN
20%
RM20
PULANGAN TUNAI
hotlink
FIBER
POSTPAID
PUSAT PENJAJA LORONG CATHAY
hotlink
QRM 5113

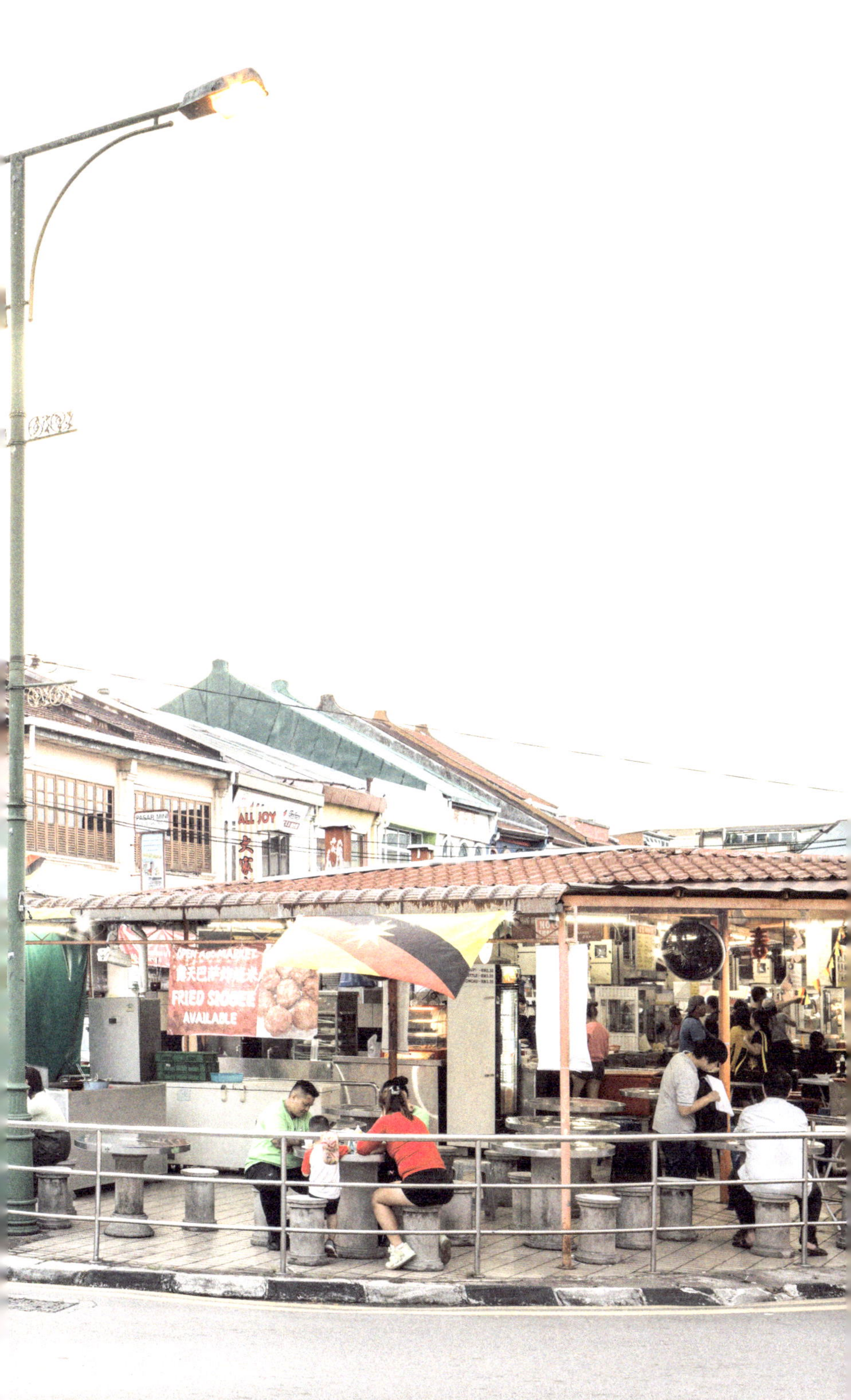
ALL JOY
FRIED
AVAILABLE

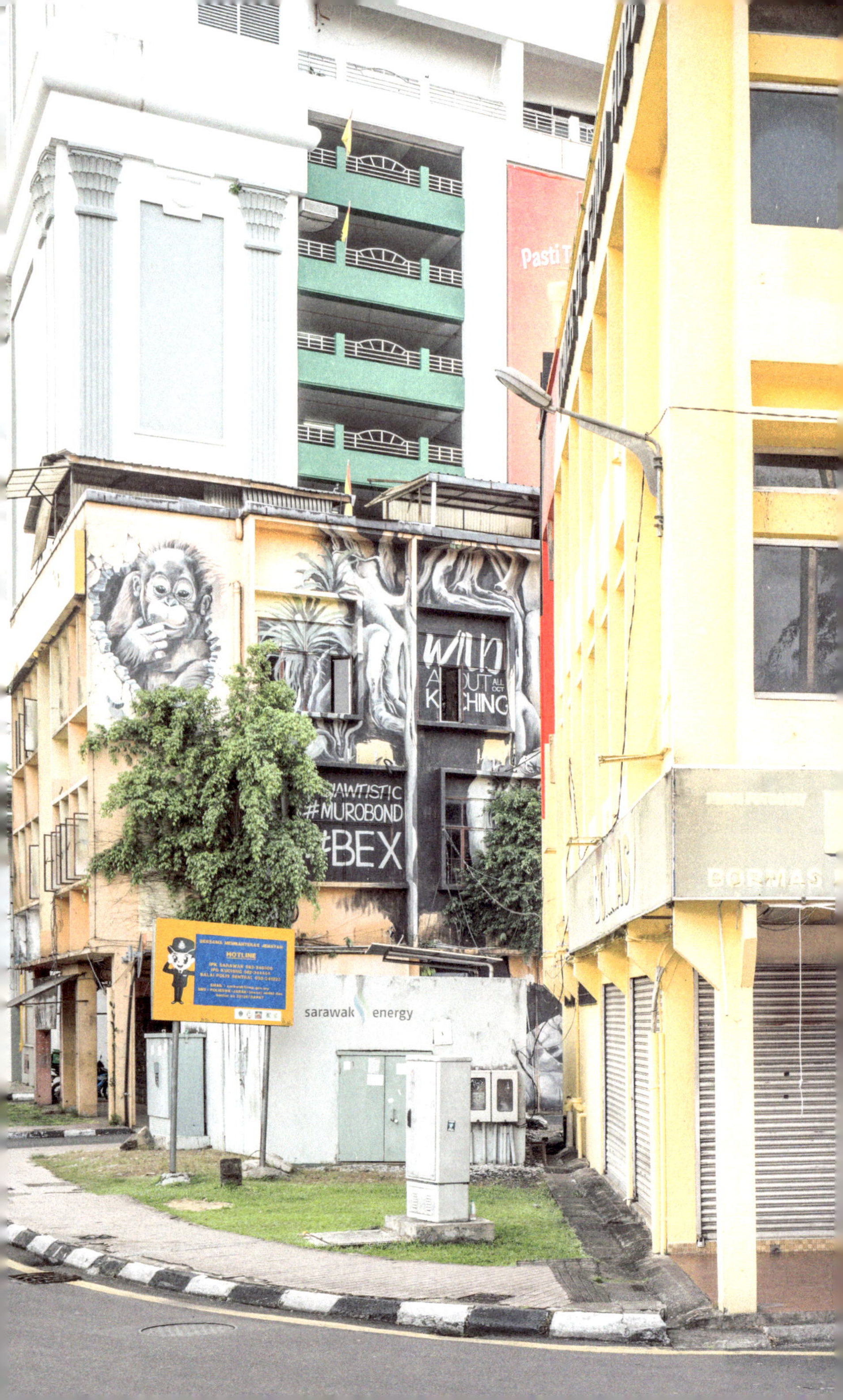
#MUROBOND
HOTLINE
sarawak energy
DORMAS

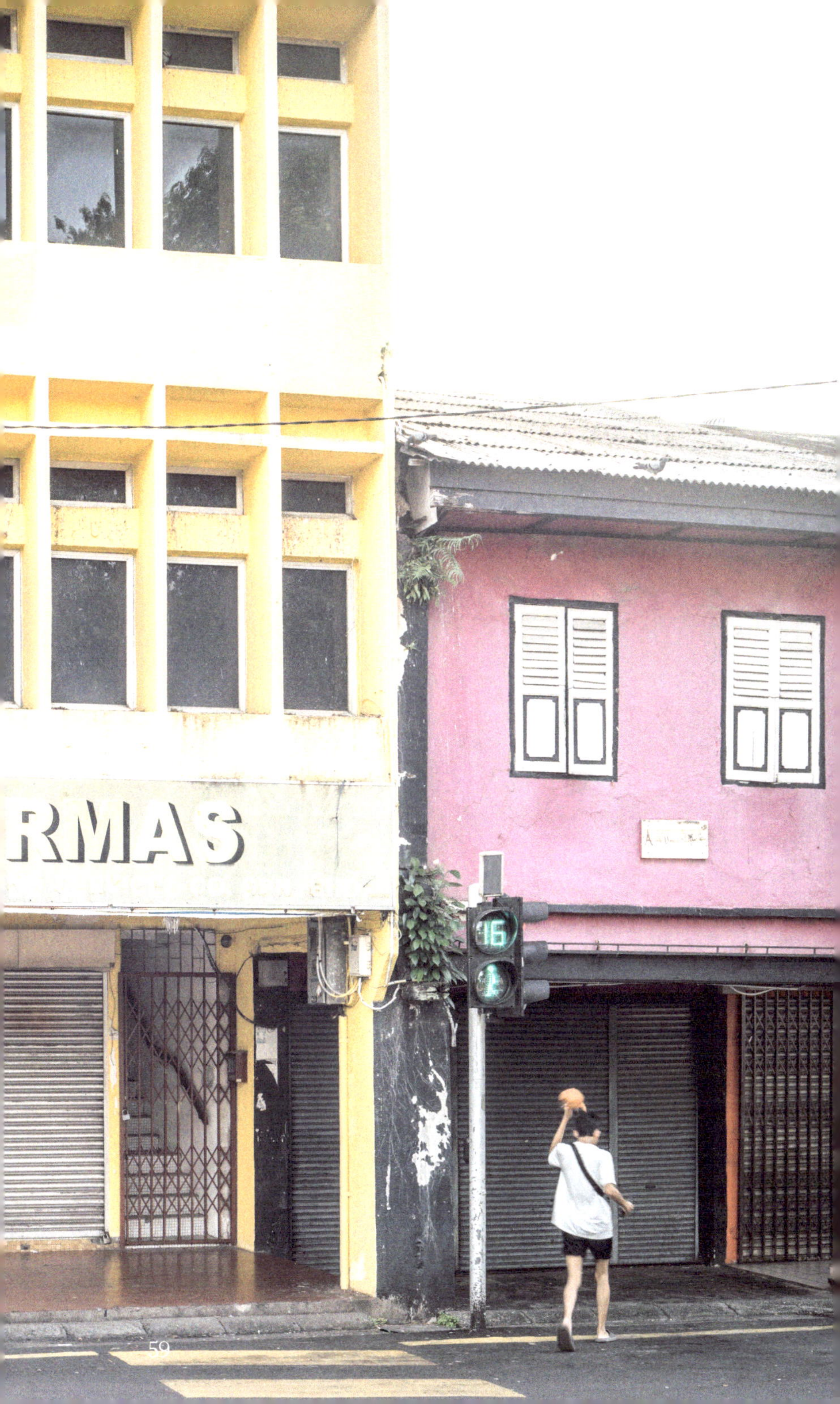
RMAS
16

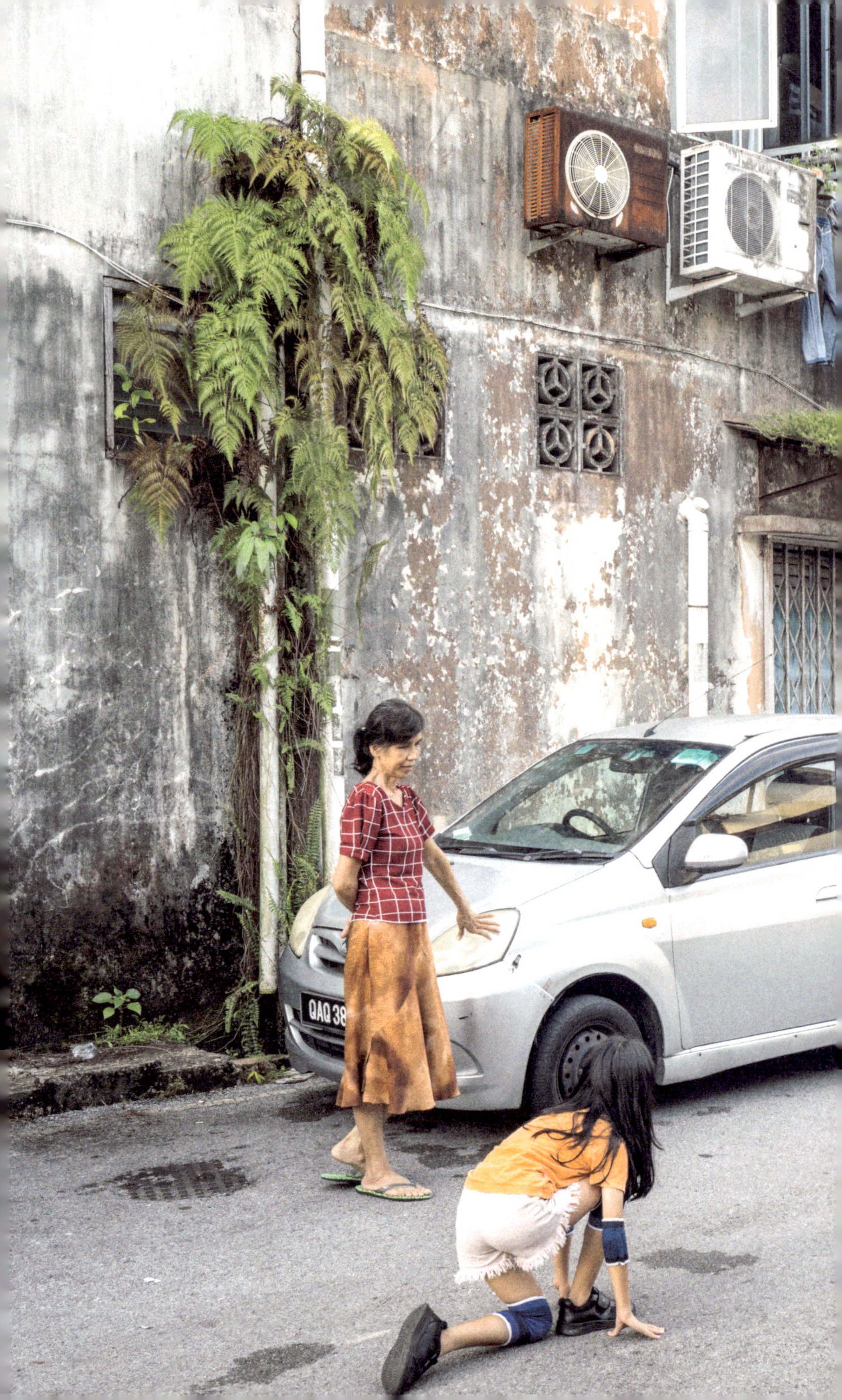
QAQ 38

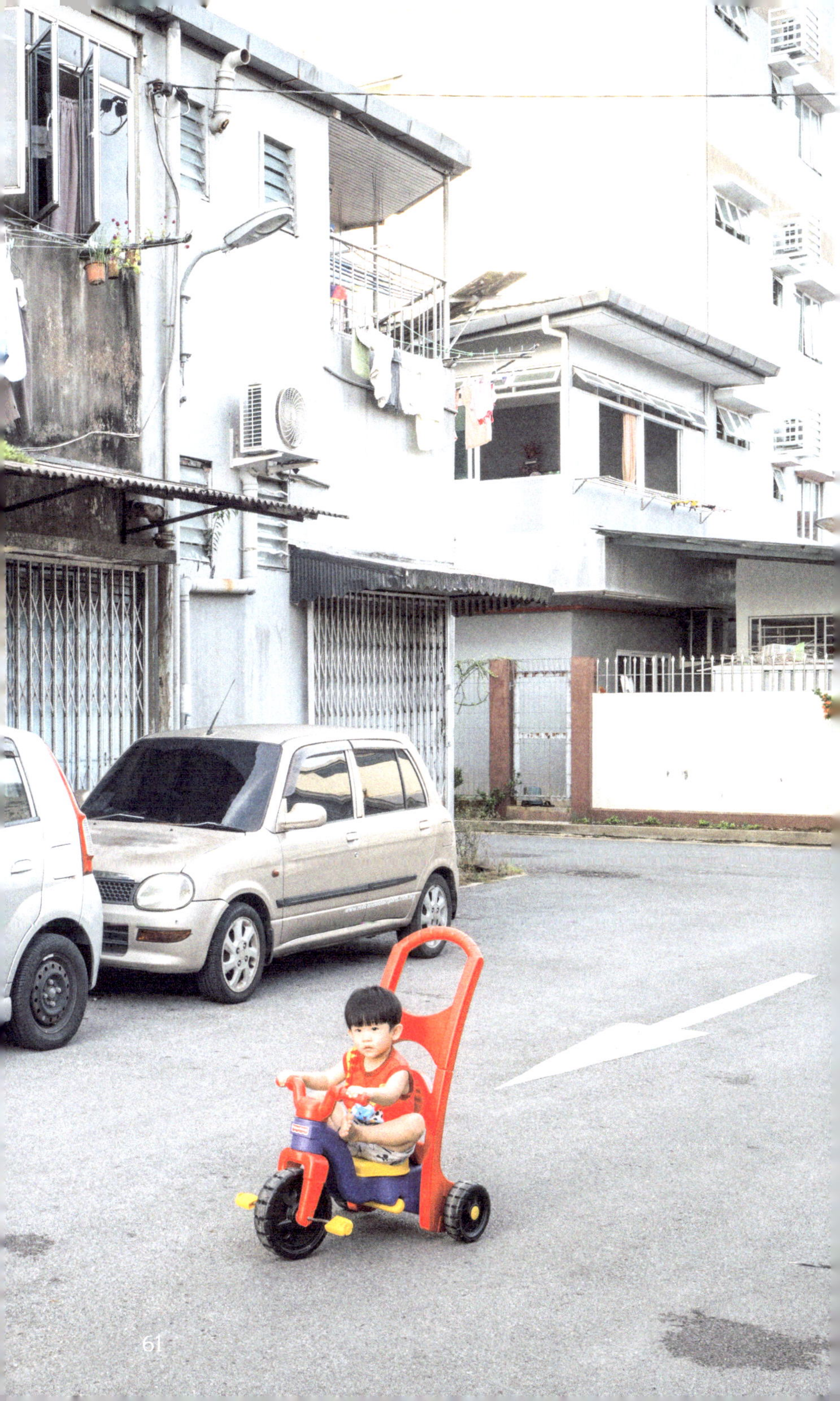

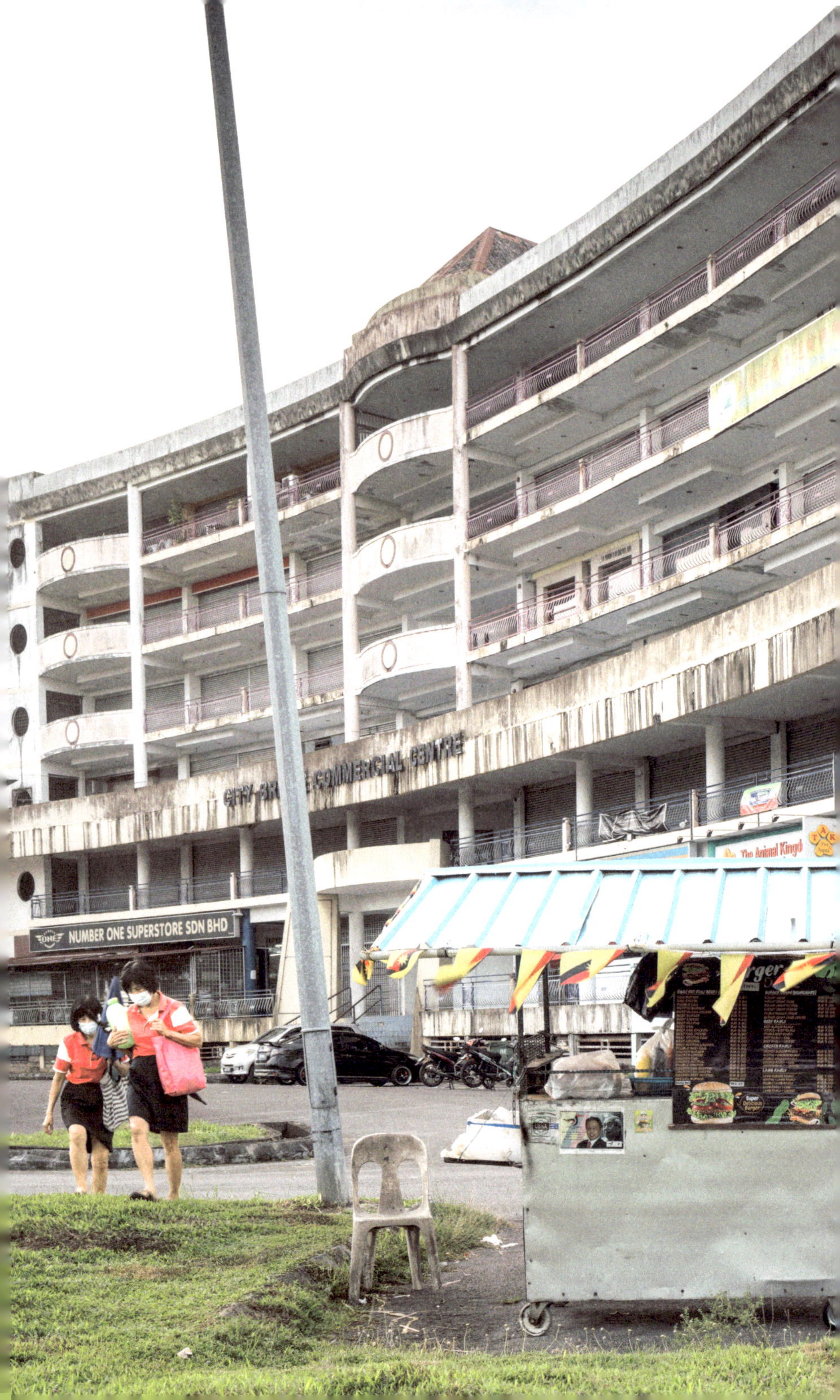
COMMERCIAL CENTRE
NUMBER ONE SUPERSTORE SDN BHD

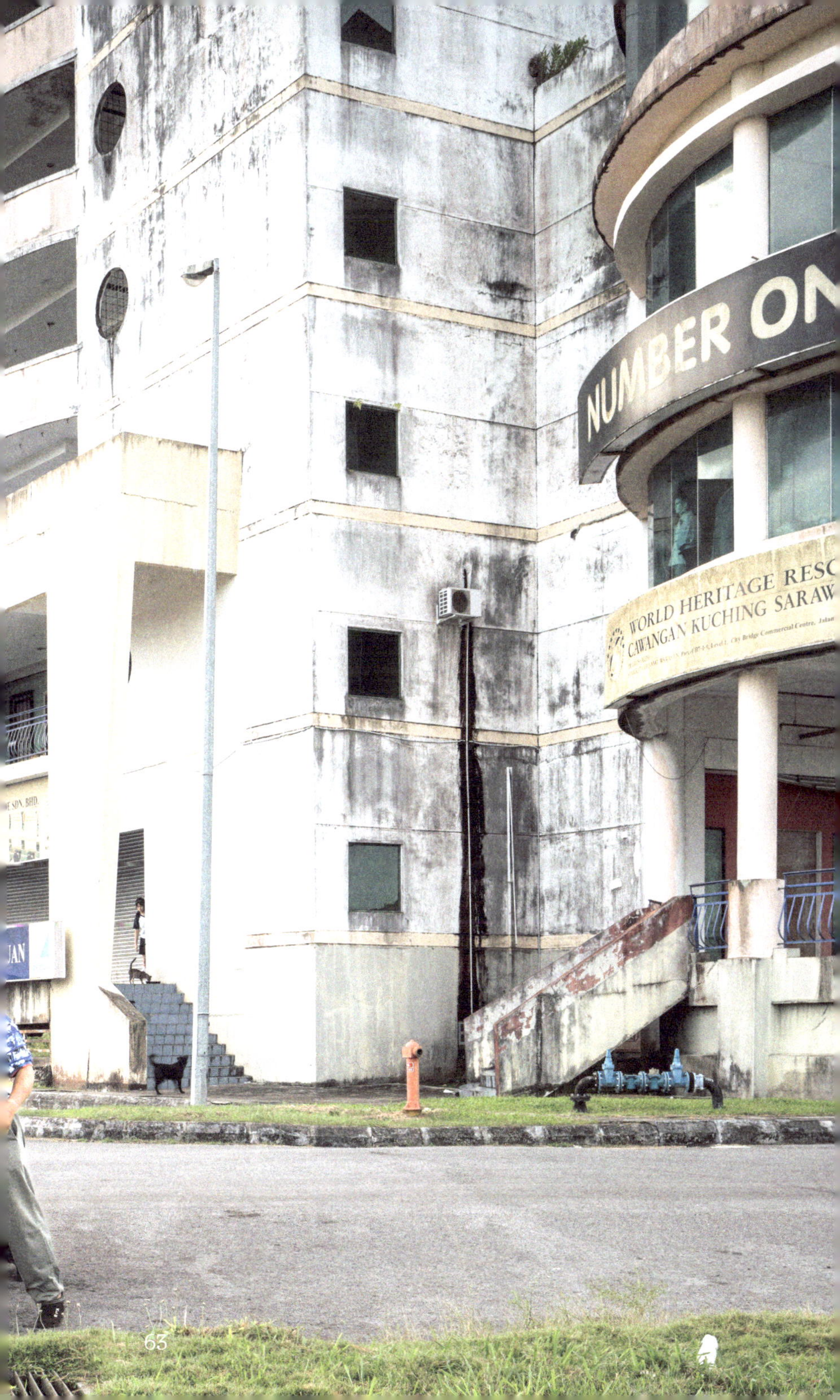
NUMBER ON
WORLD HERITAGE RESO
CAWANGAN KUCHING SARAW
E SDN. BHD.
JAN

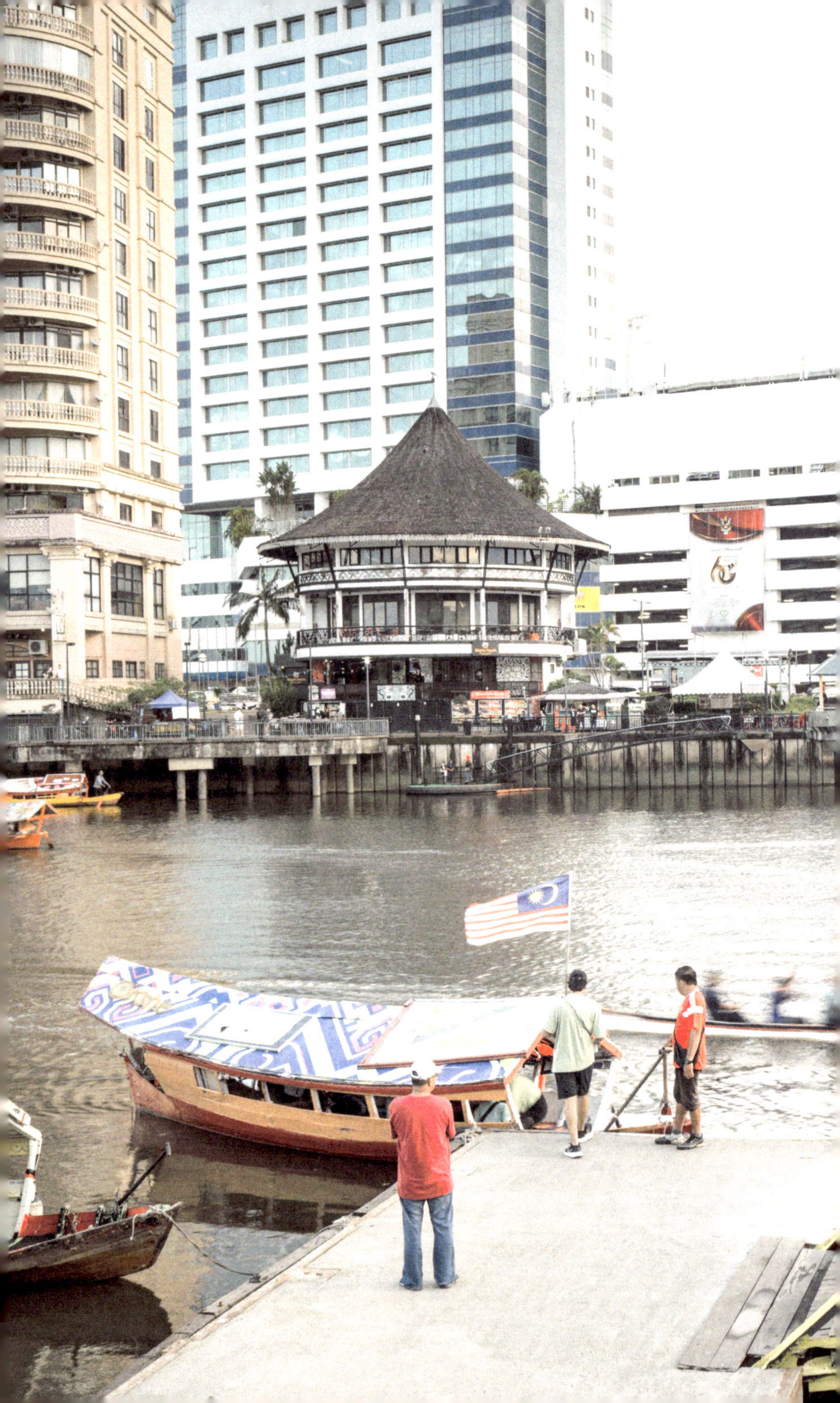

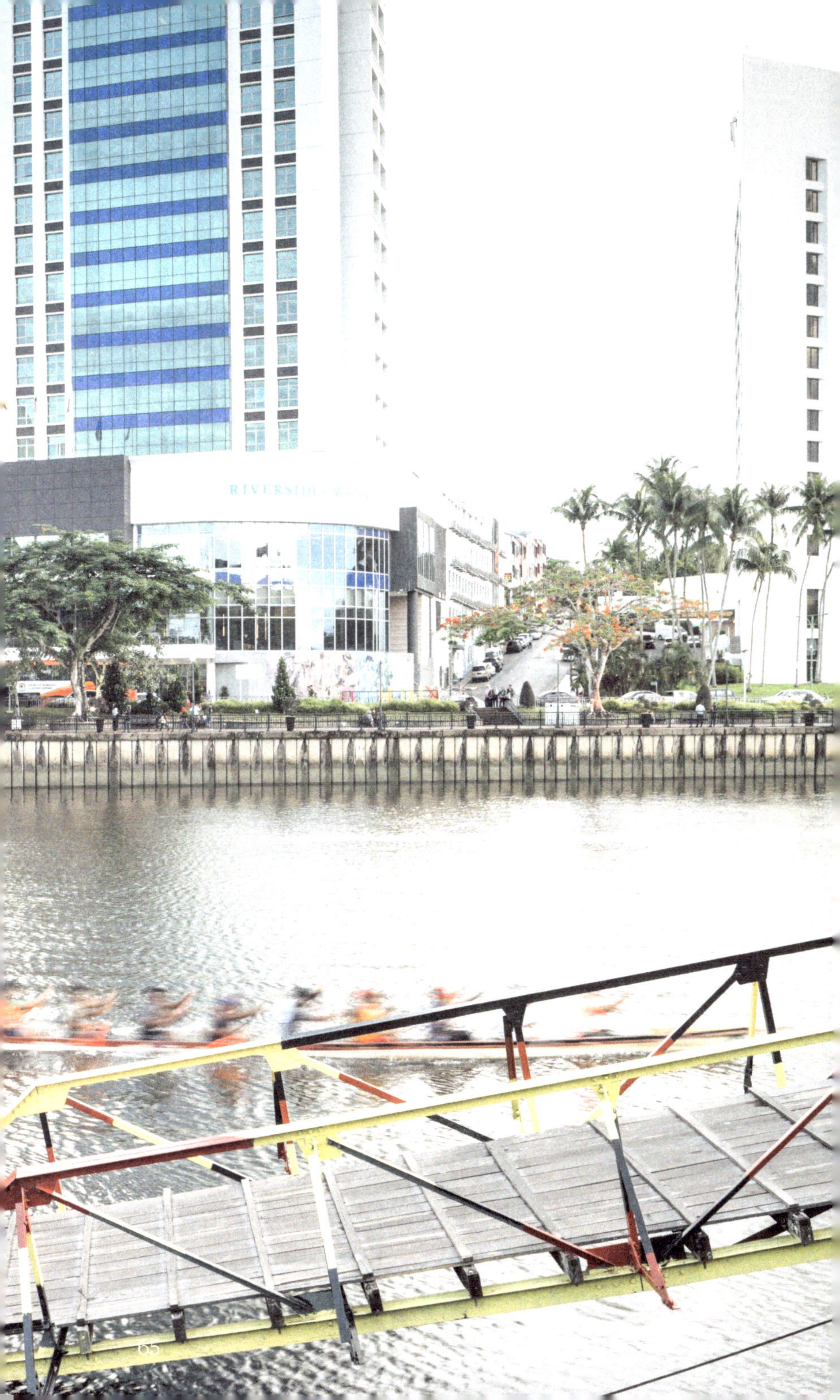

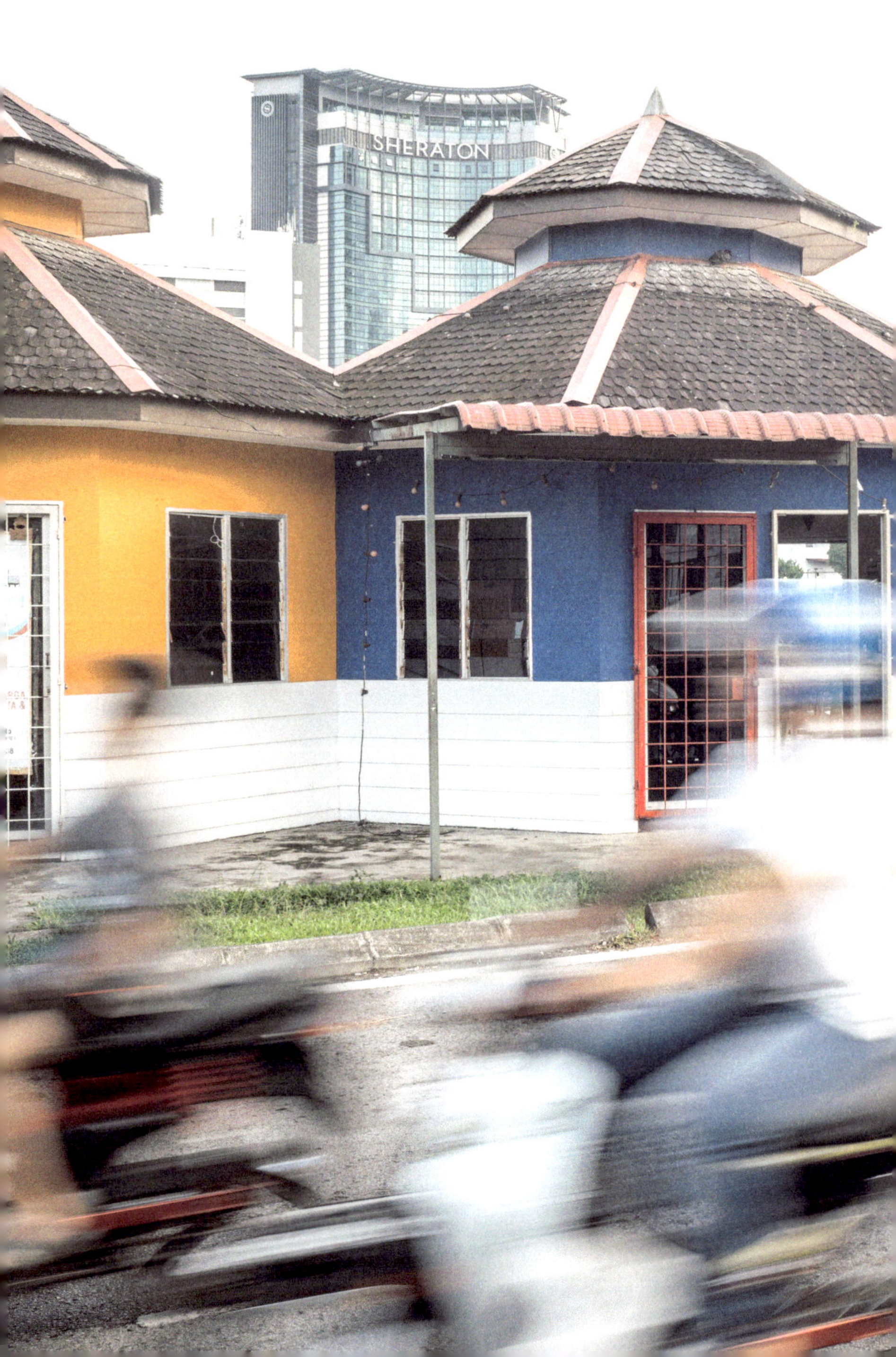
SHERATON

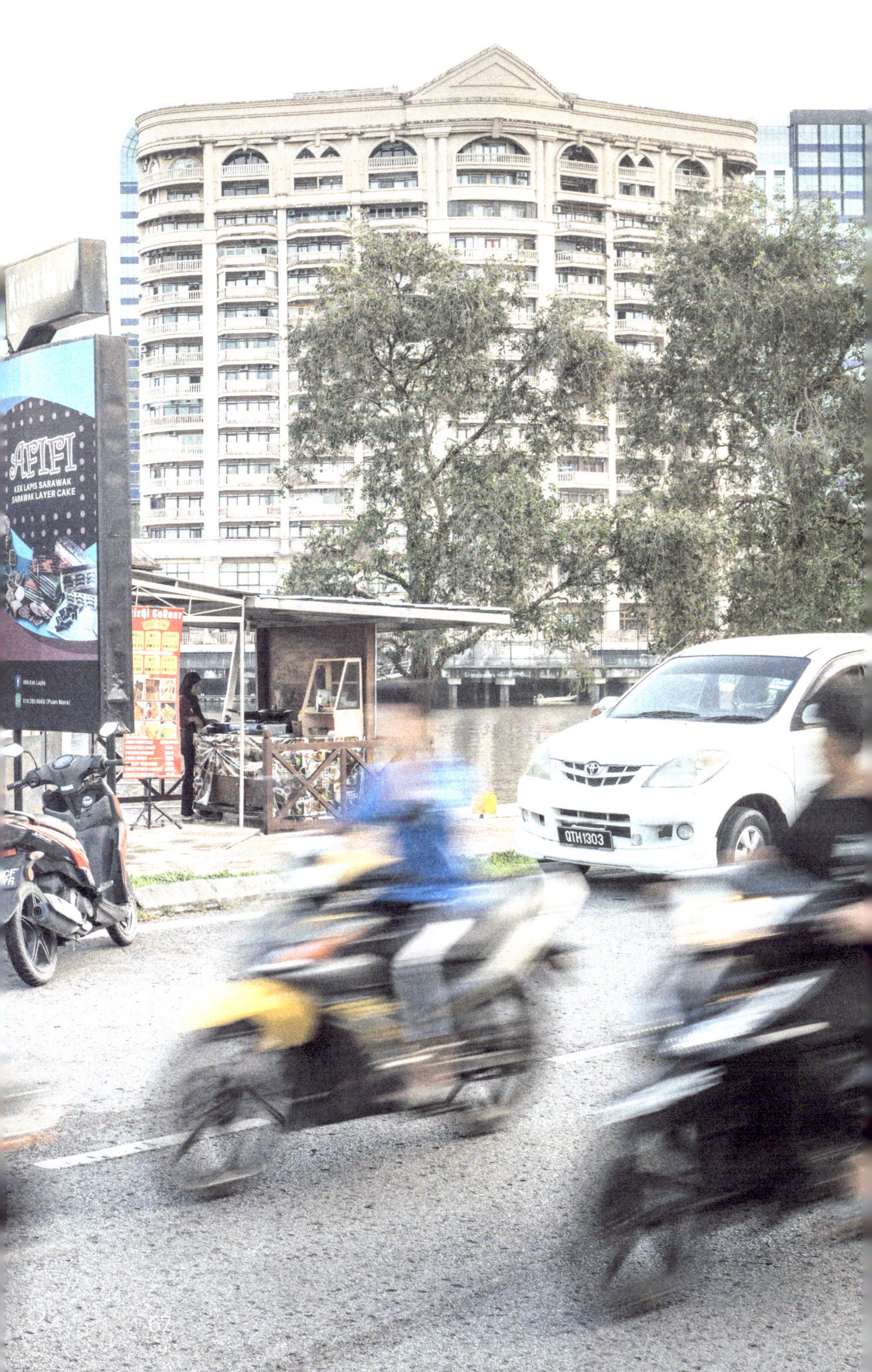
AFIFI
KEK LAPIS SARAWAK
SARAWAK LAYER CAKE
QTH1303

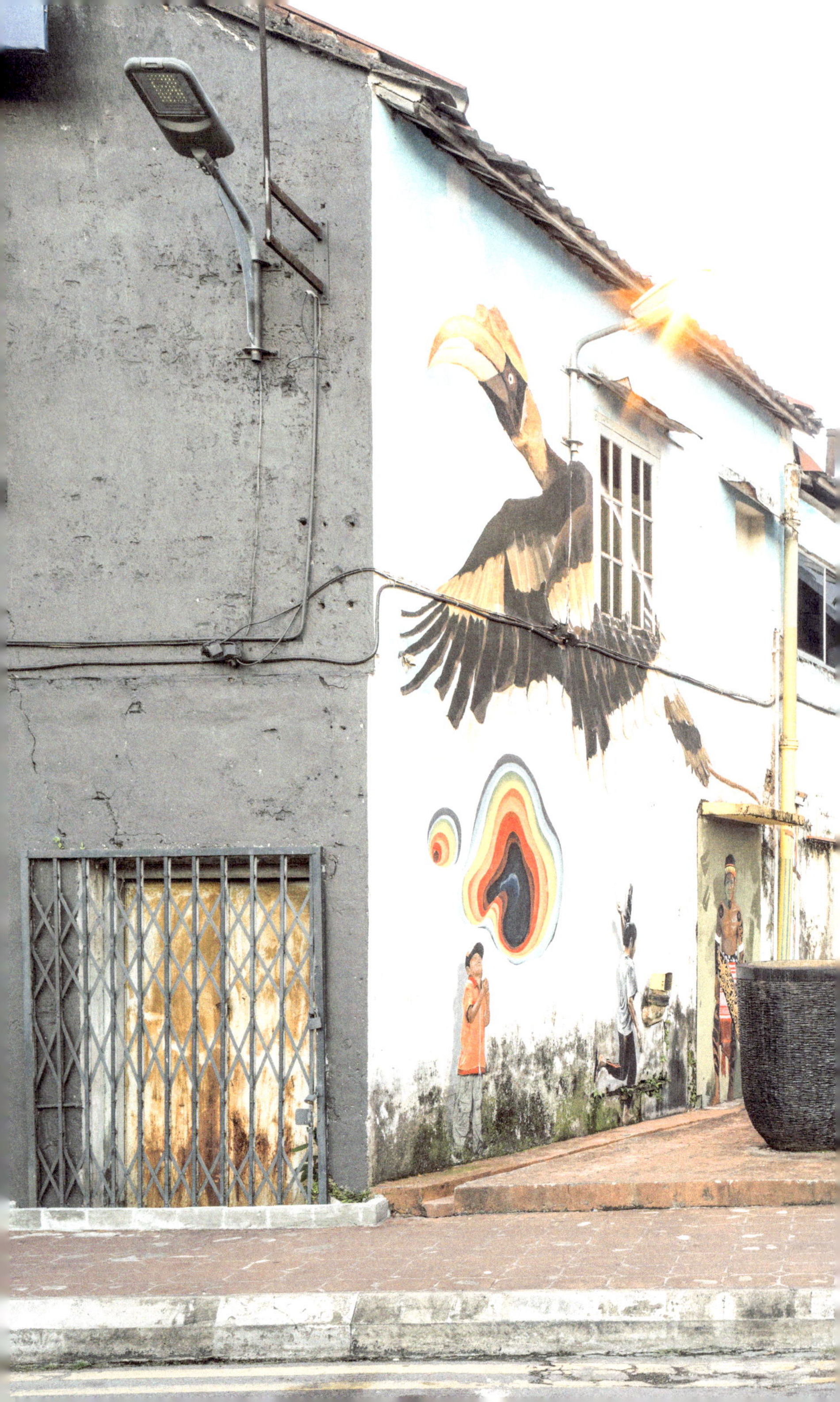

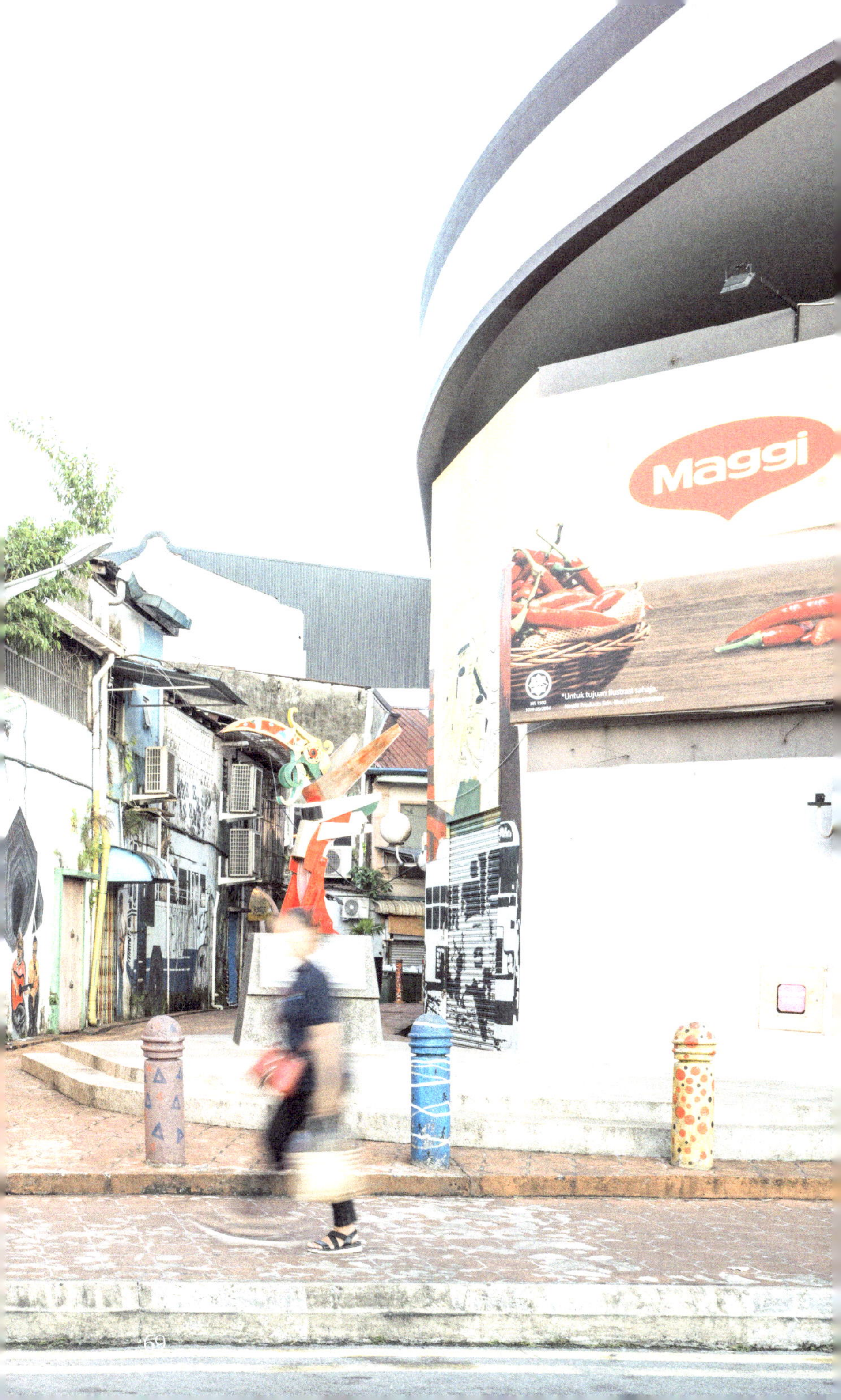
Maggi
MS 1500
*Untuk tujuan ilustrasi sahaja.

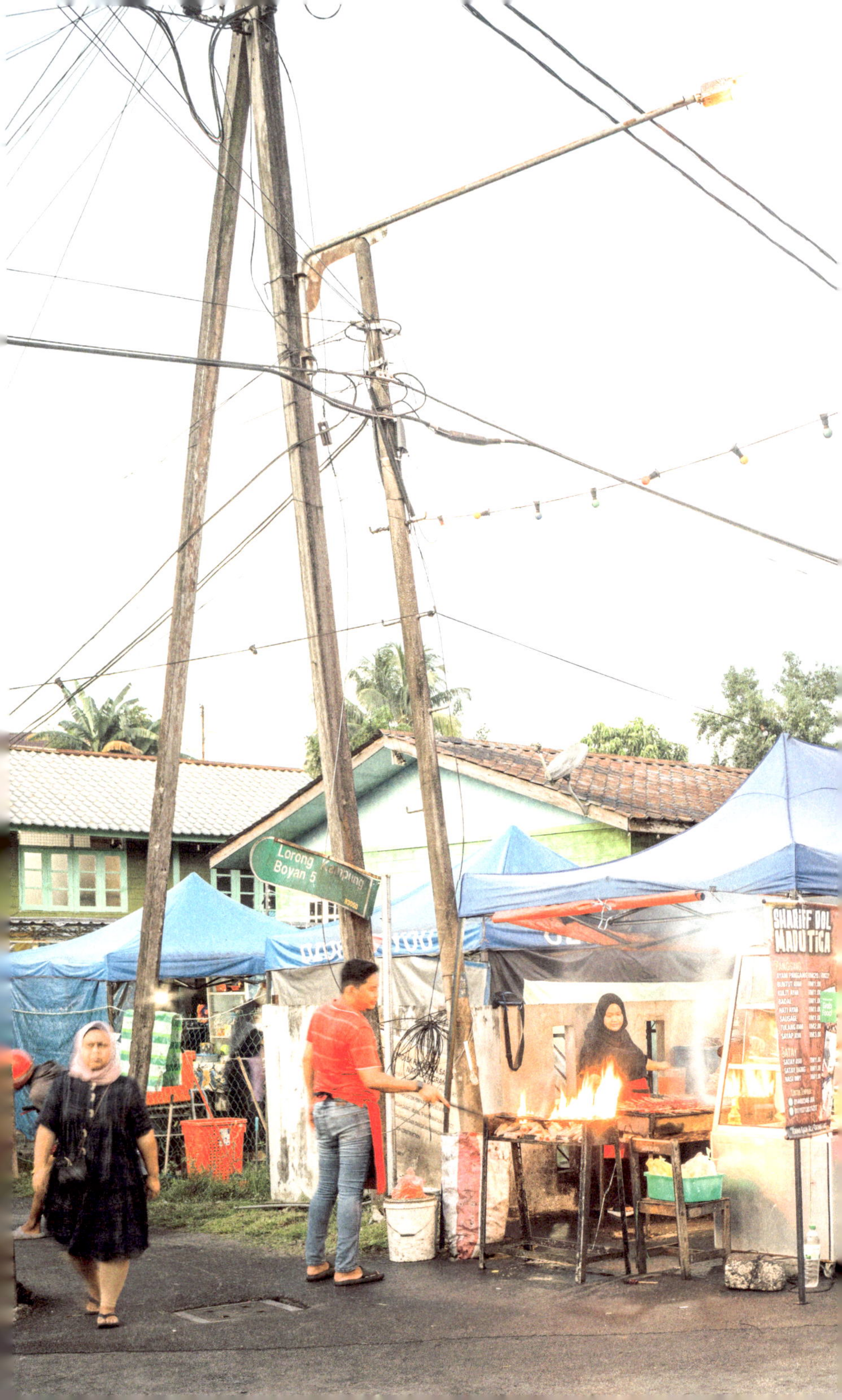
Lorong Kampung
Boyan 5
SHARIFF DOL
MADU TIGA

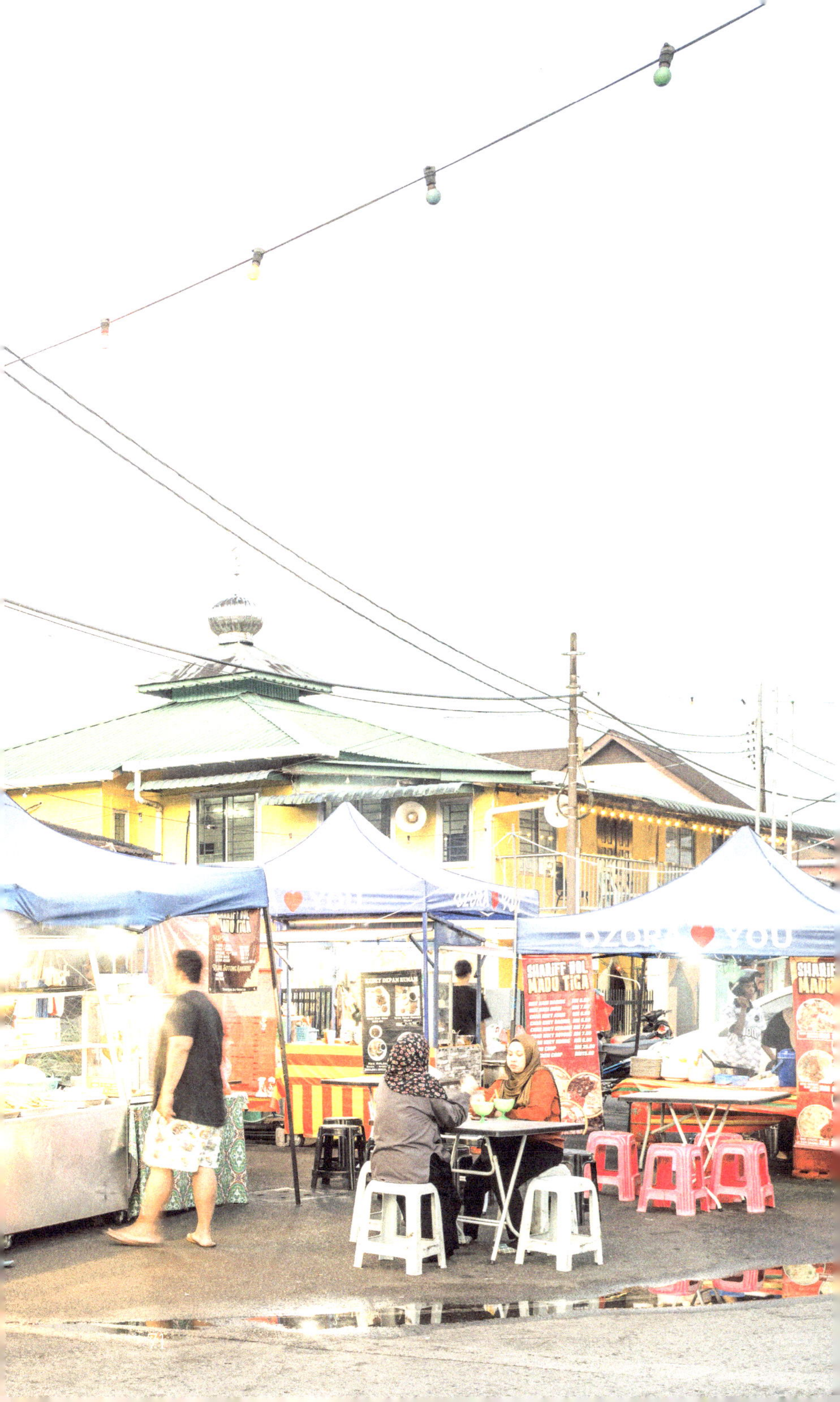
SHARIFF DOL
MADU TIGA
YOU

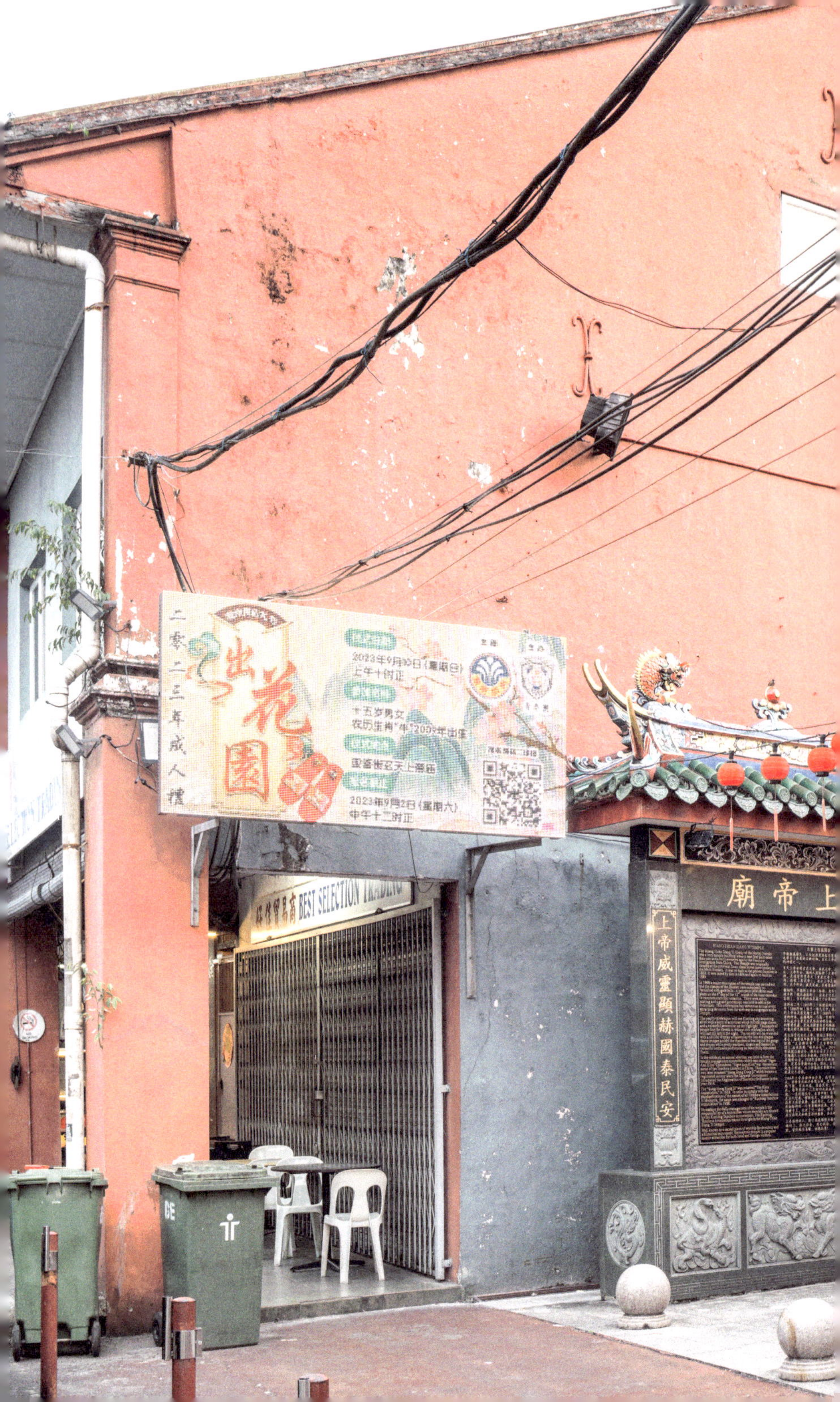
二零二三年成人禮
出花園
2023年9月10日(星期日)
上午十时正
十五岁男女
2023年9月2日(星期六)
中午十二时正
BEST SELECTION TRADING
上帝廟
上帝威靈顯赫國泰民安

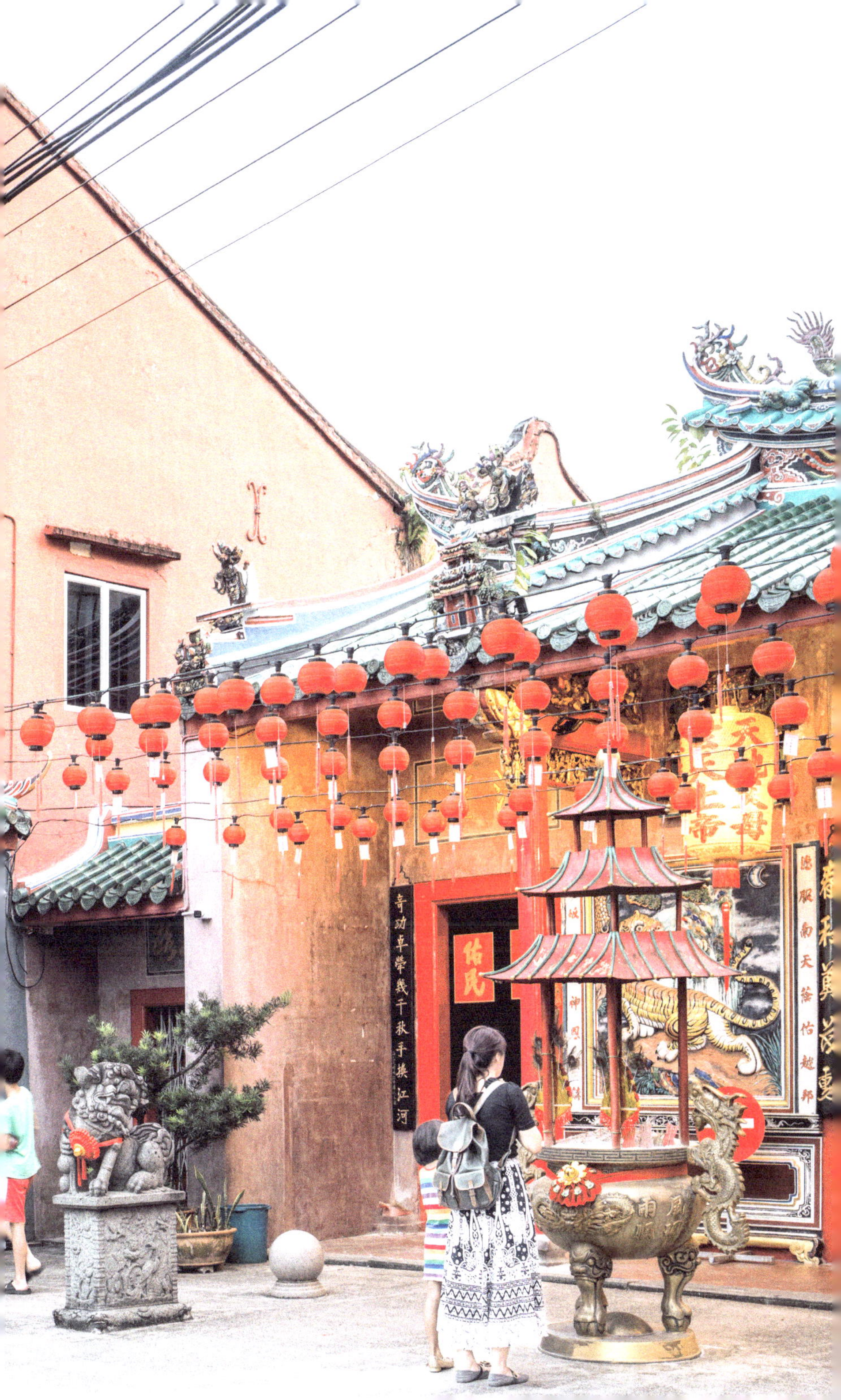
奇功卓犖幾千秋手換江河
佑民
德服南天蔭佑越邦

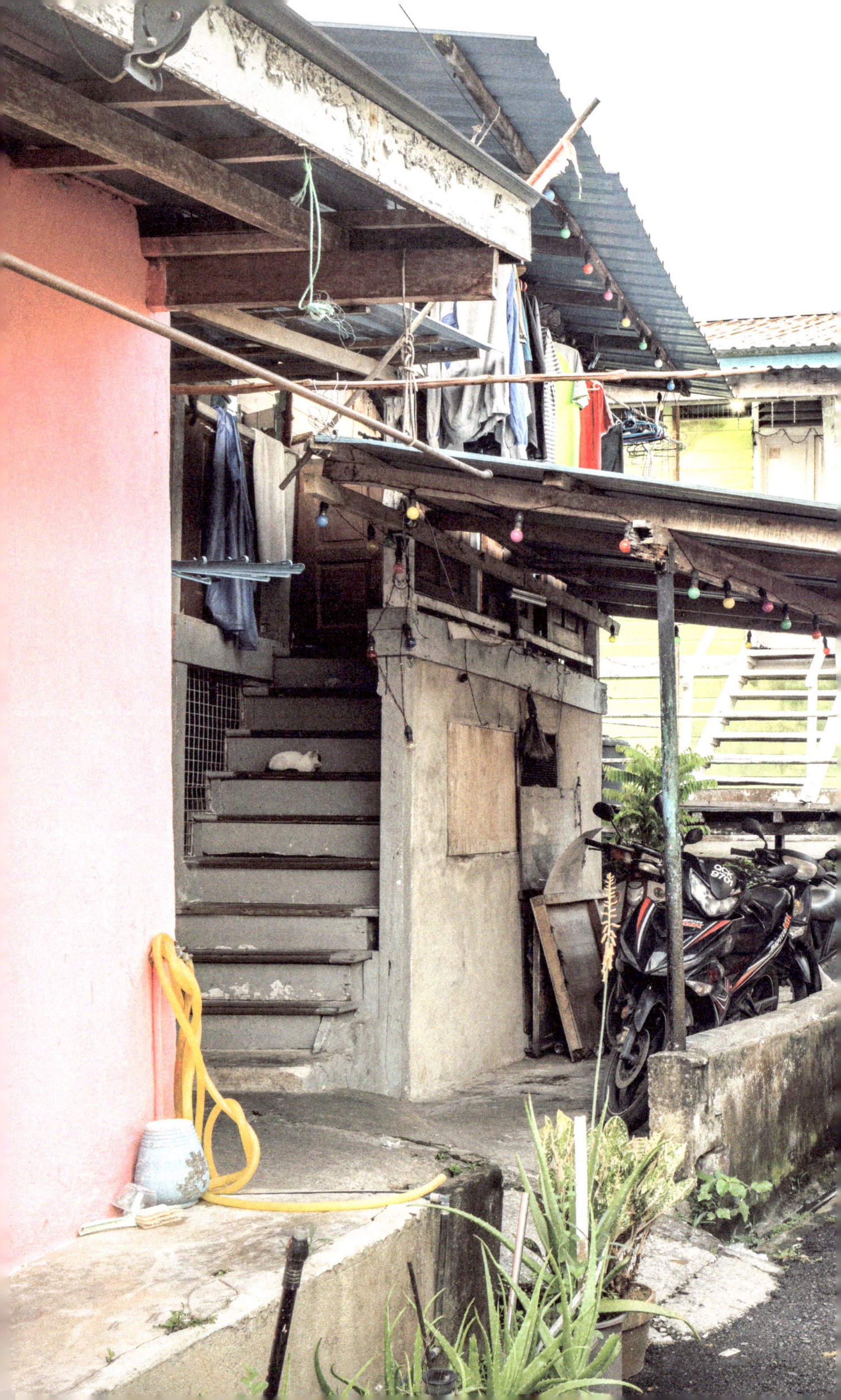
QCK
9701
JUPITER MX

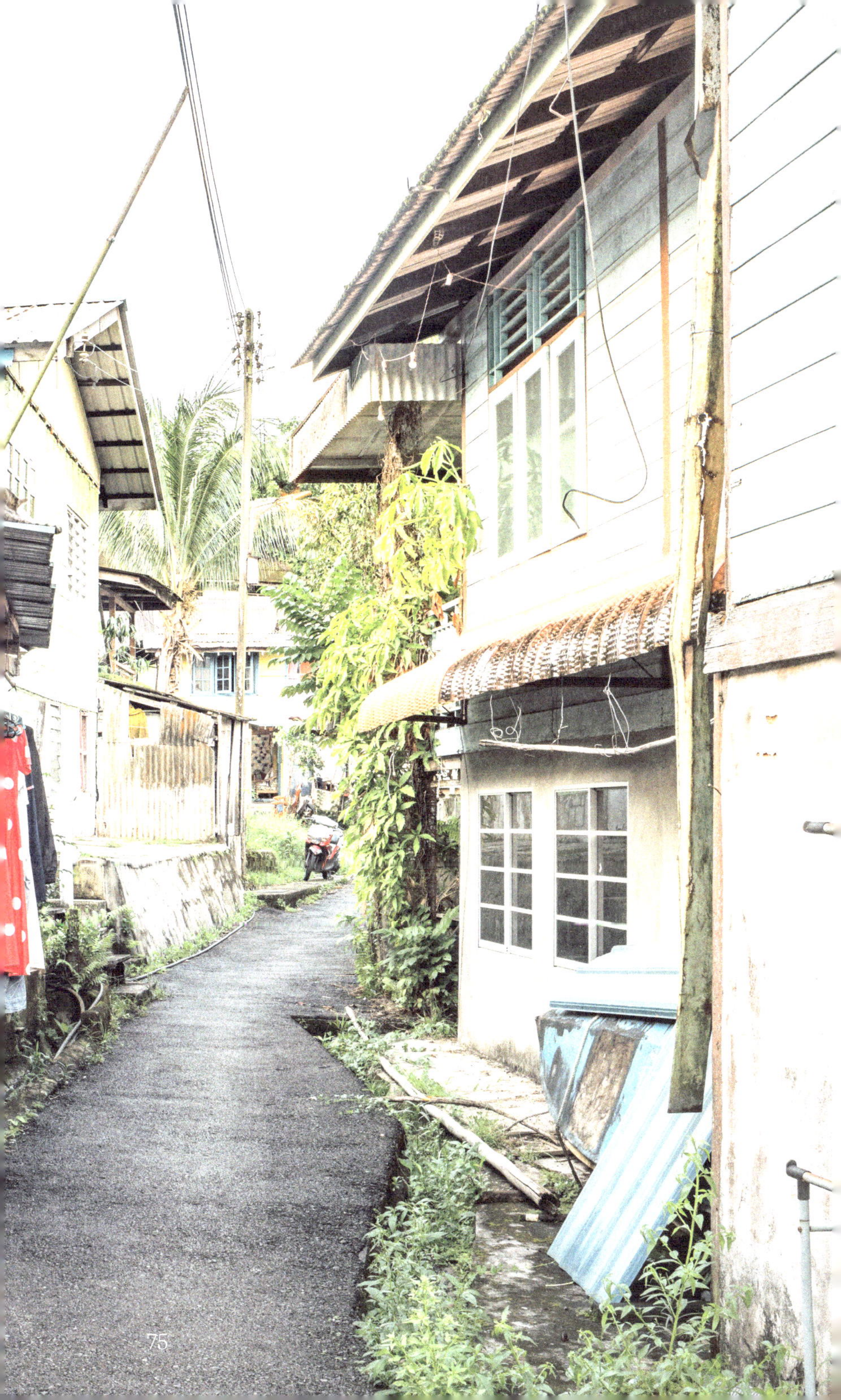

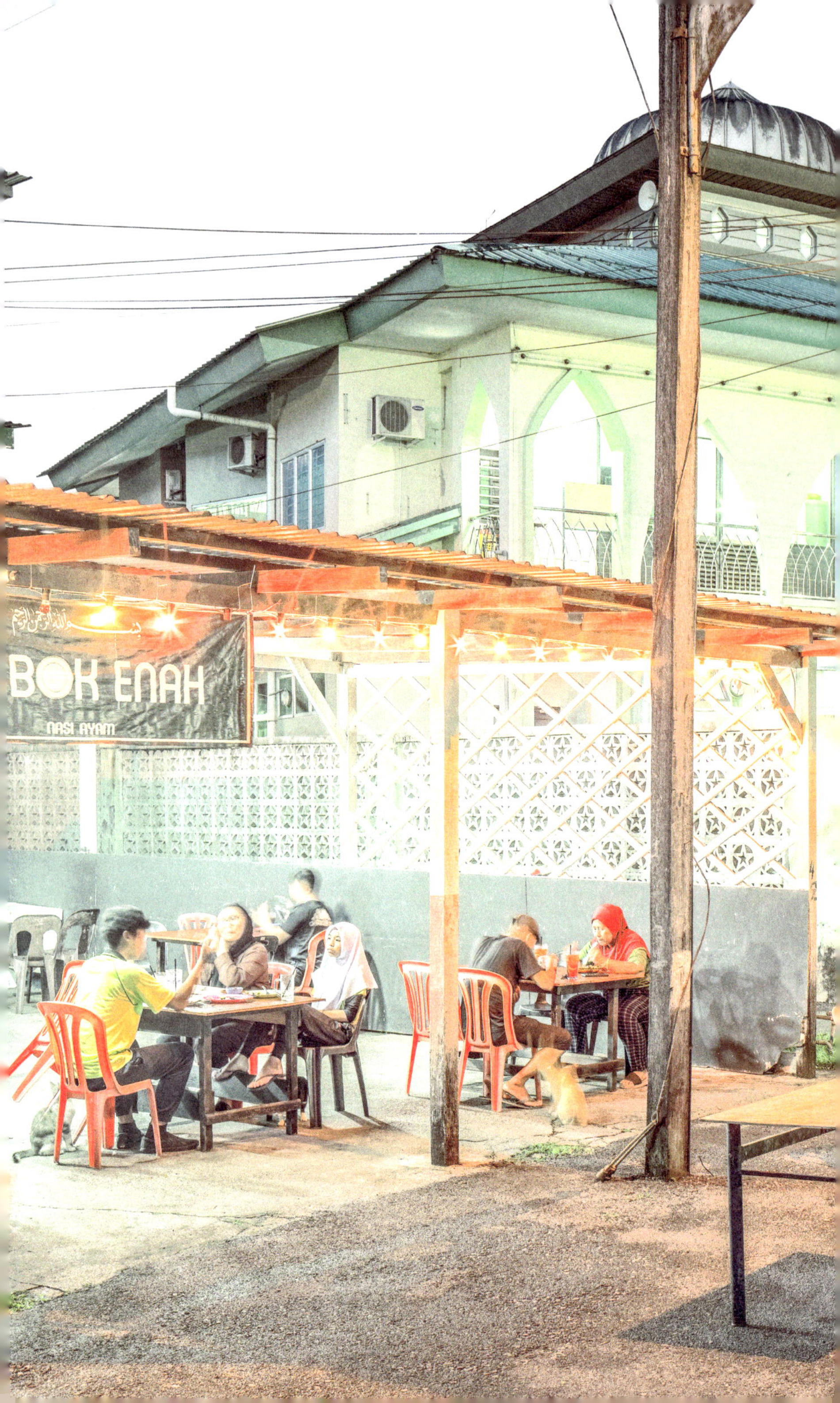
BOK ENAH
NASI AYAM

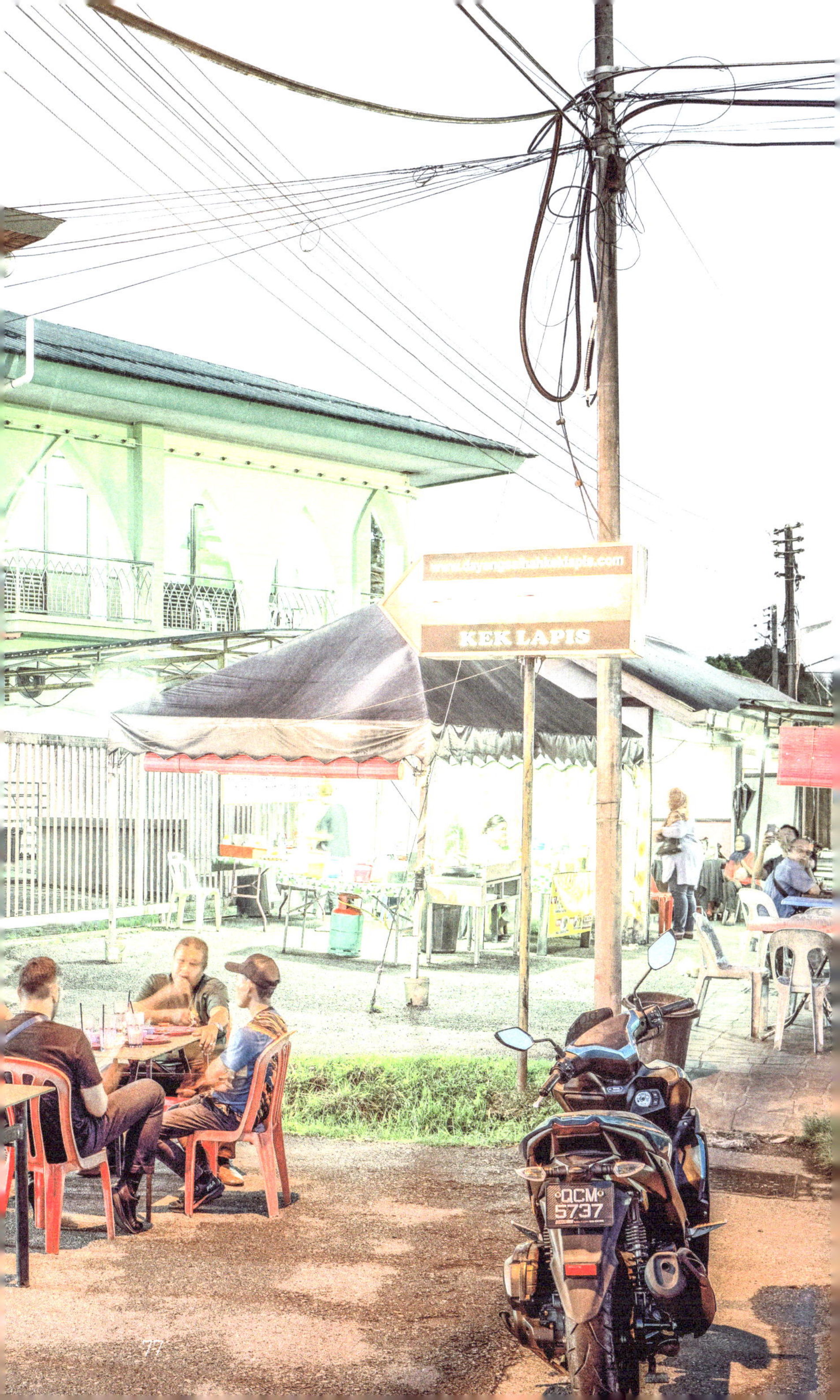
KEK LAPIS

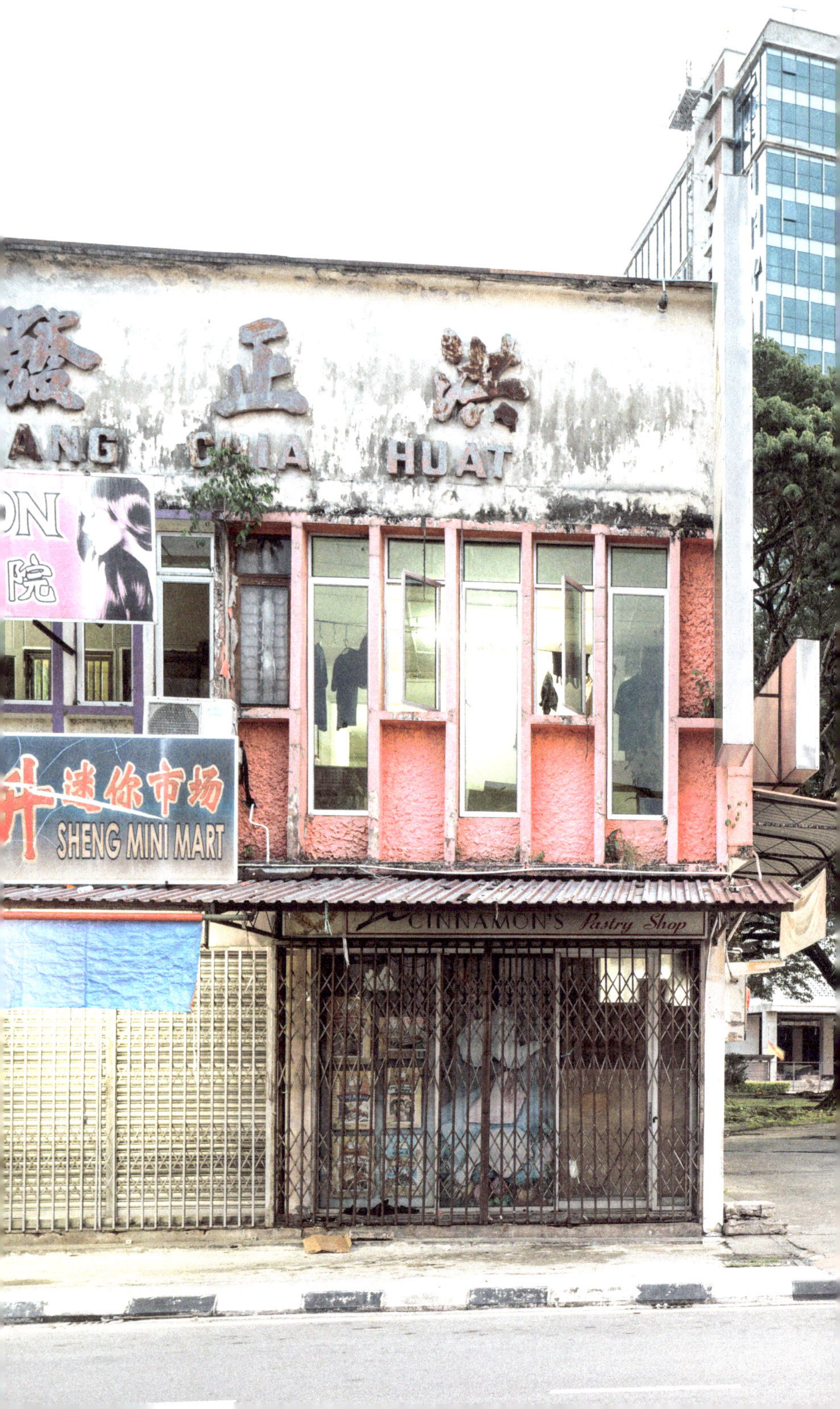

ANG CHIA HUAT
迷你市场
SHENG MINI MART
CINNAMON'S Pastry Shop

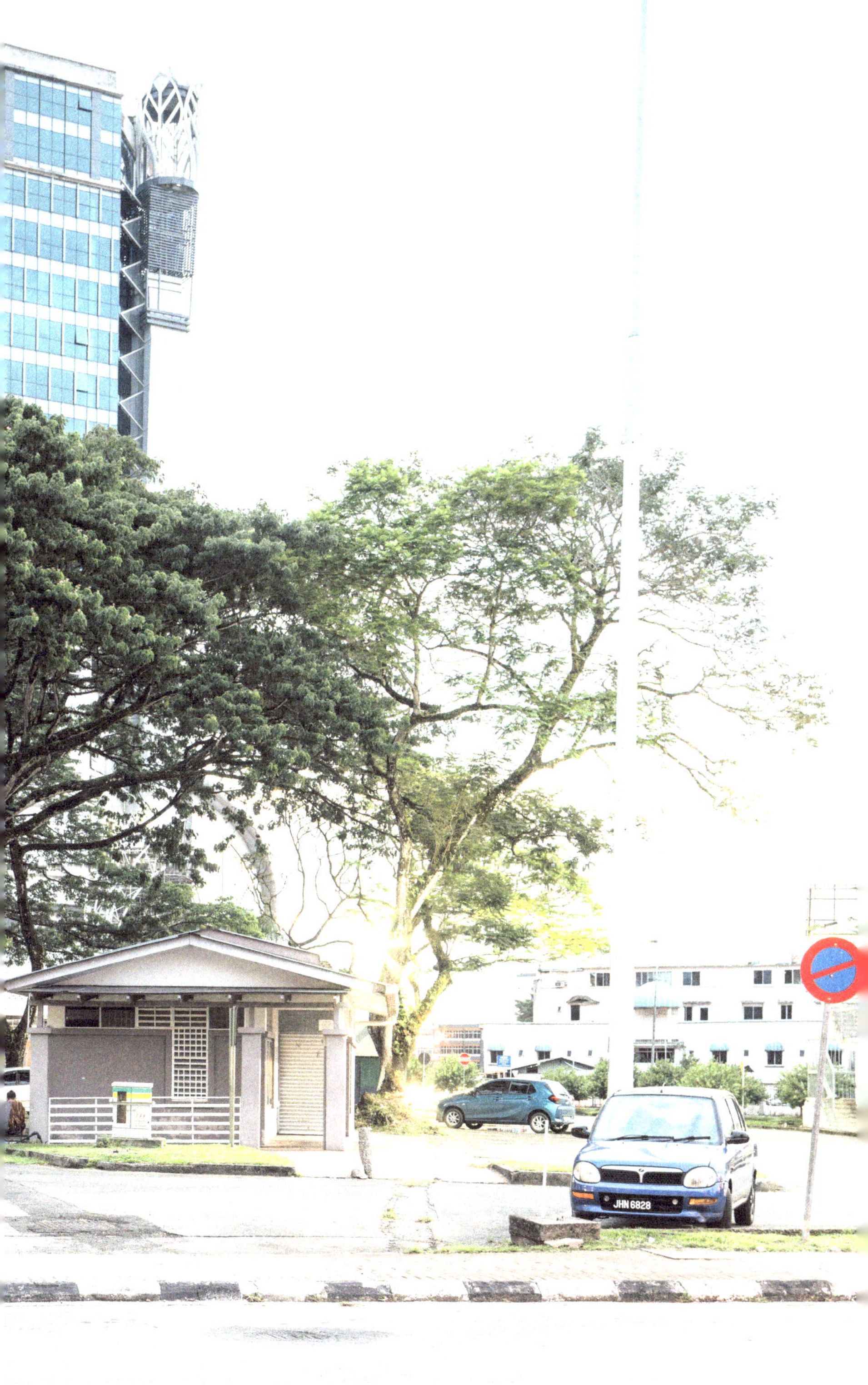
JHN 6828

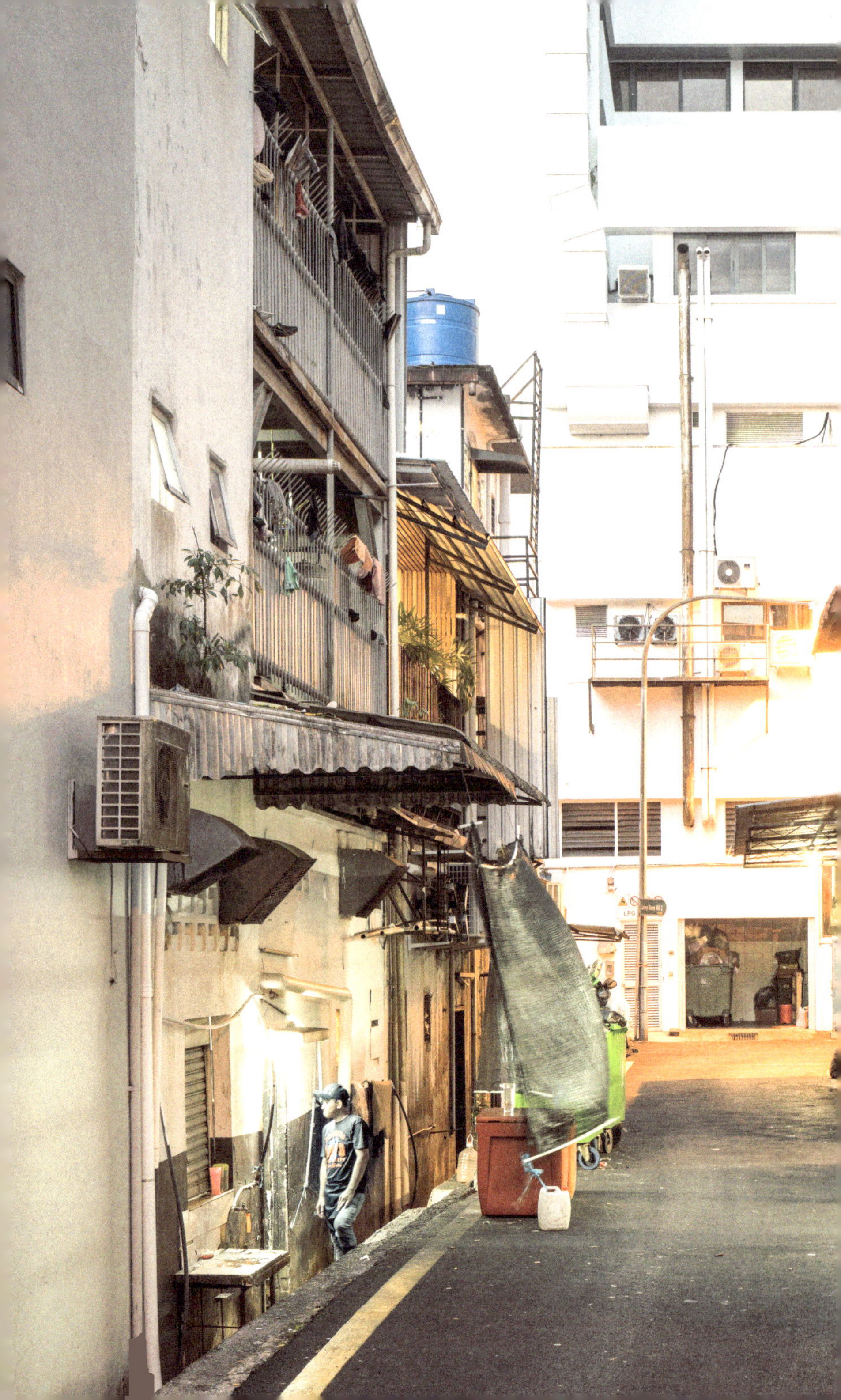
LPG

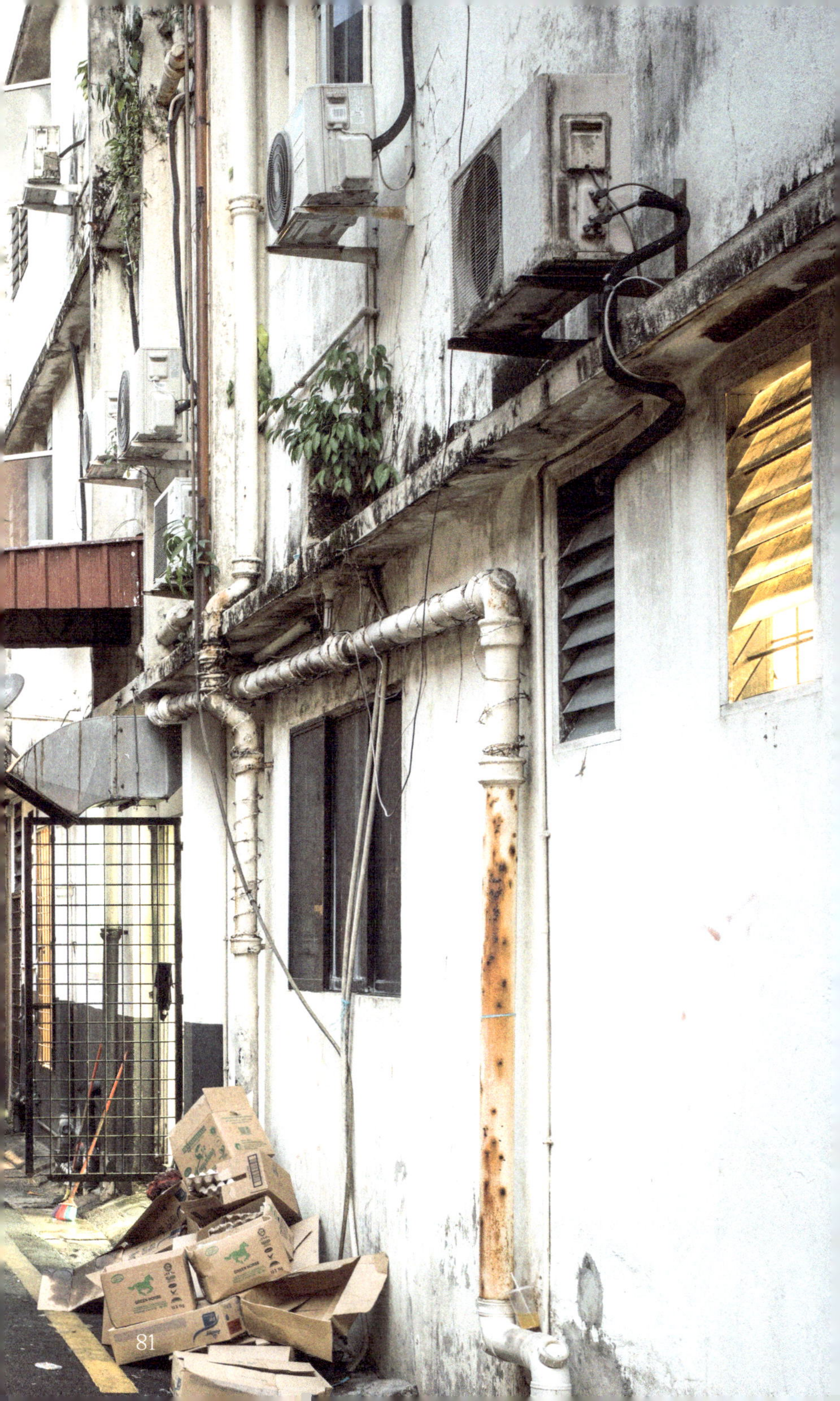

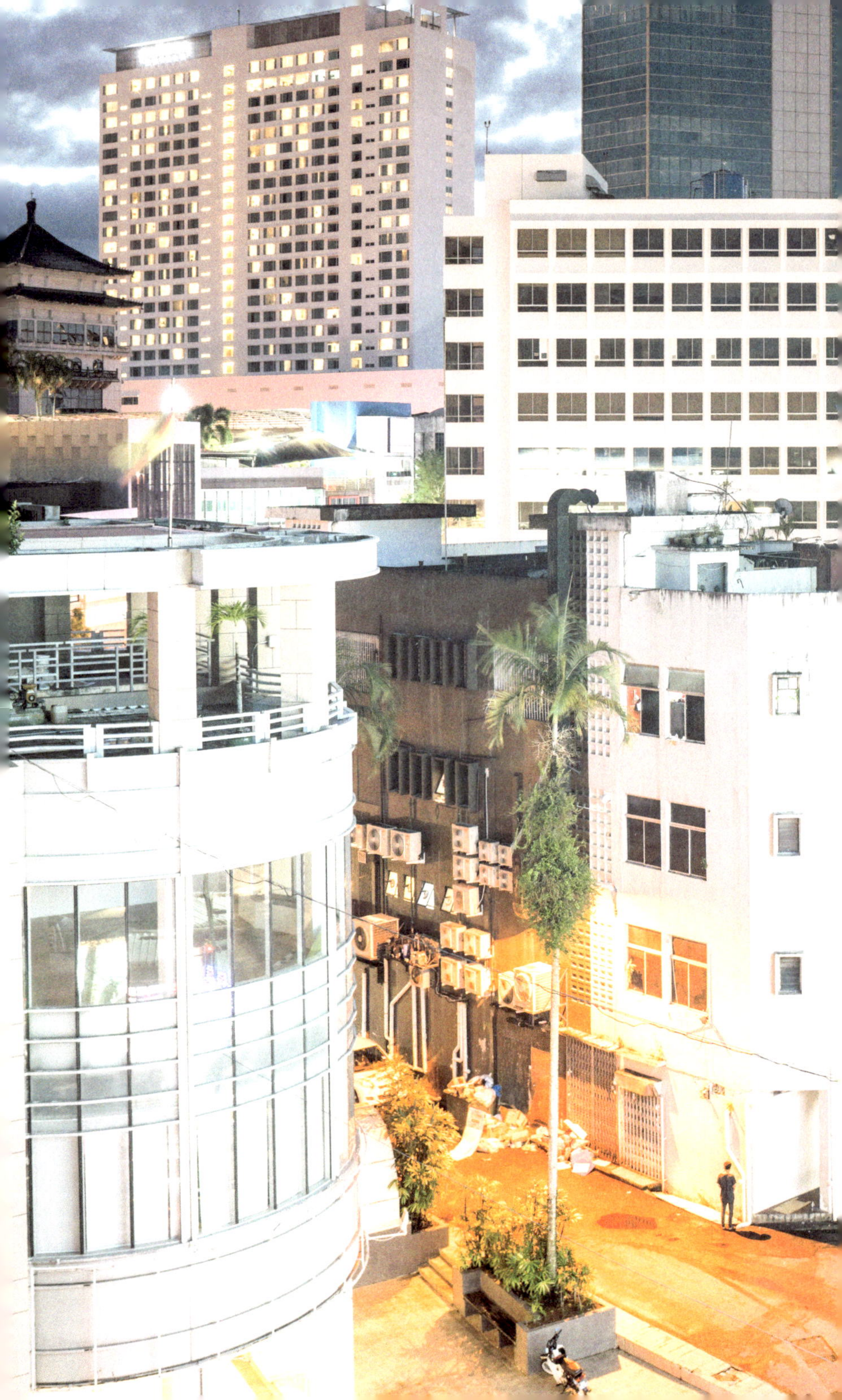

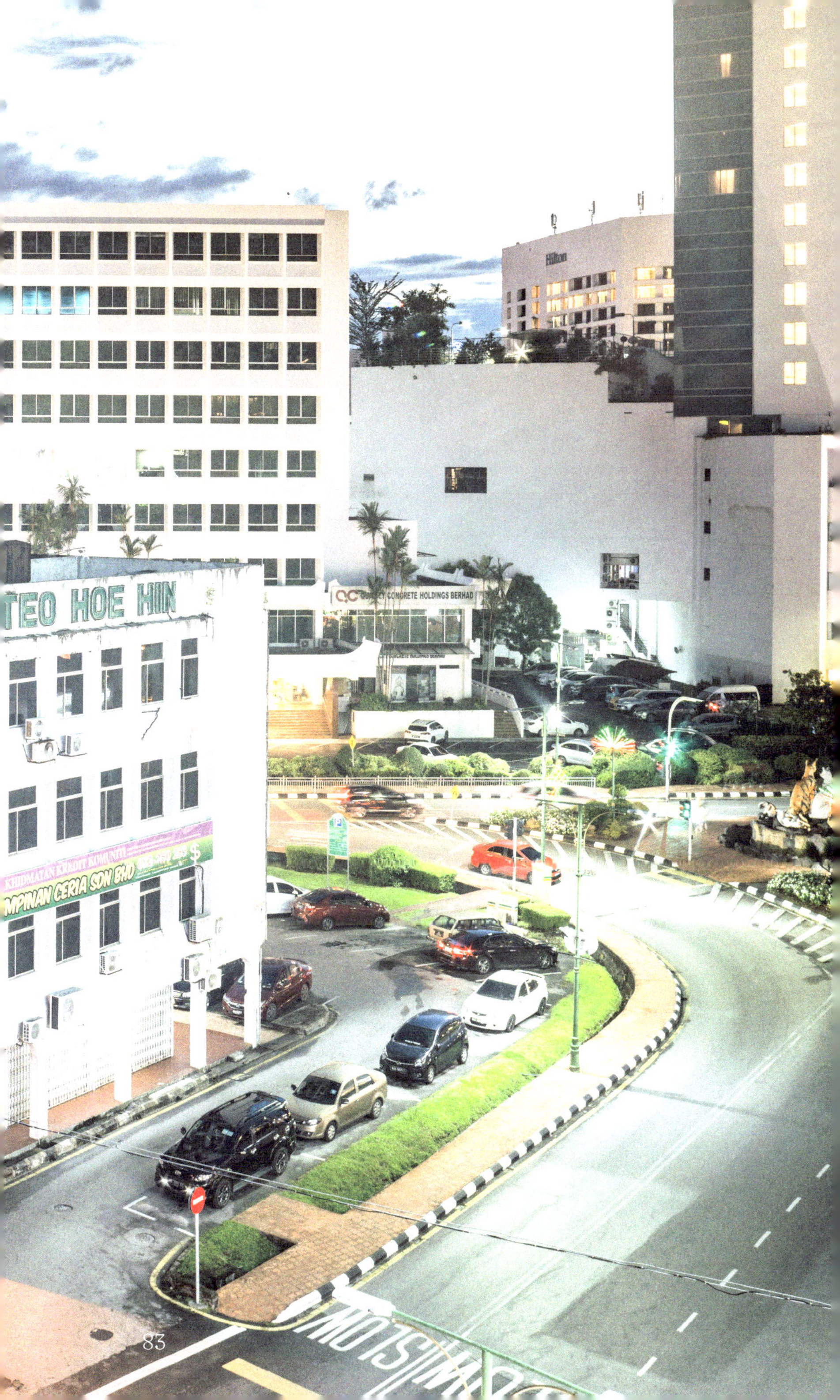
Hilton
TEO HOE HIN
CONCRETE HOLDINGS BERHAD
KHIDMATAN KREDIT KOMUNITI
MPINAN CERIA SDN BHD

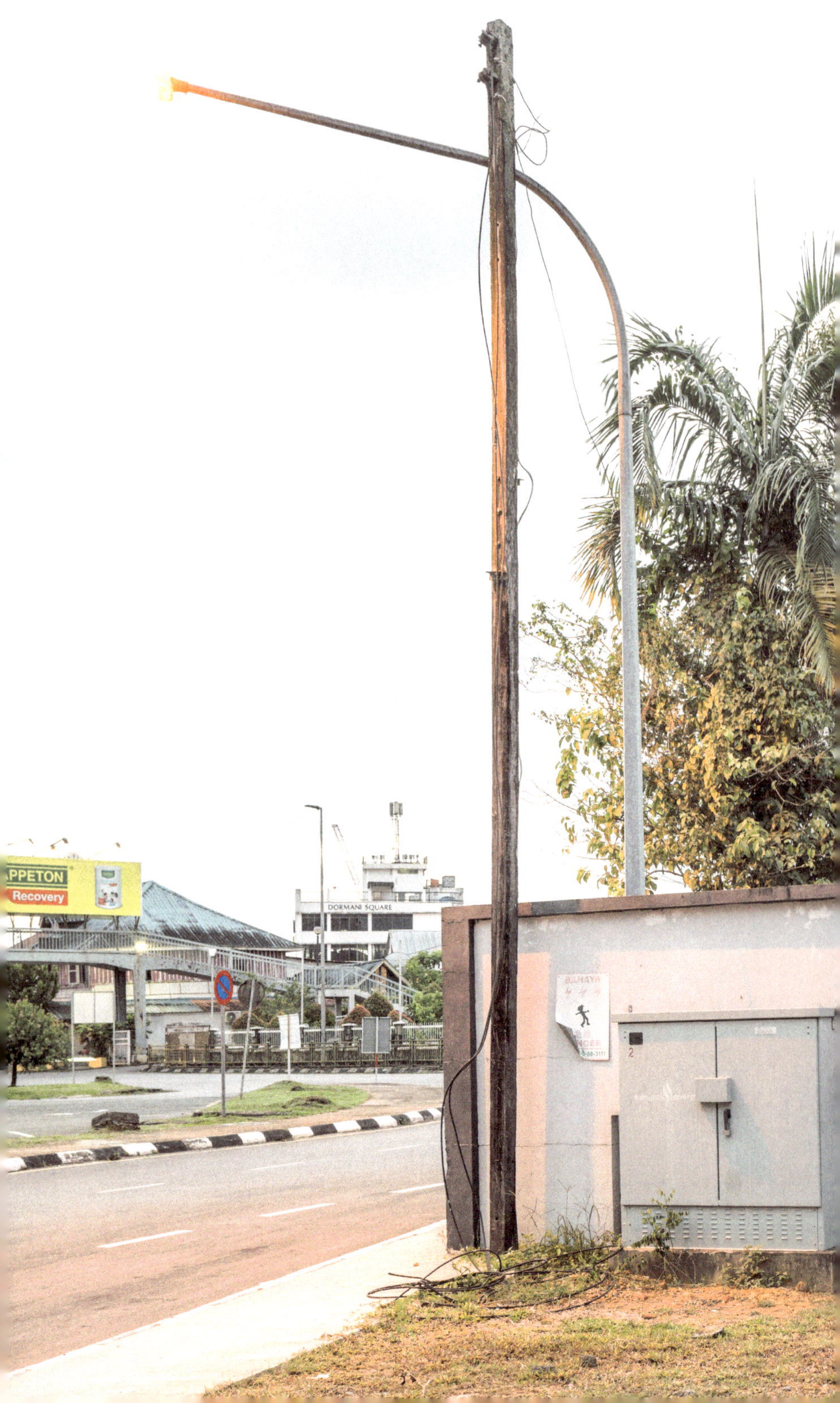
PPETON
Recovery
DORMANI SQUARE
BAHAYA

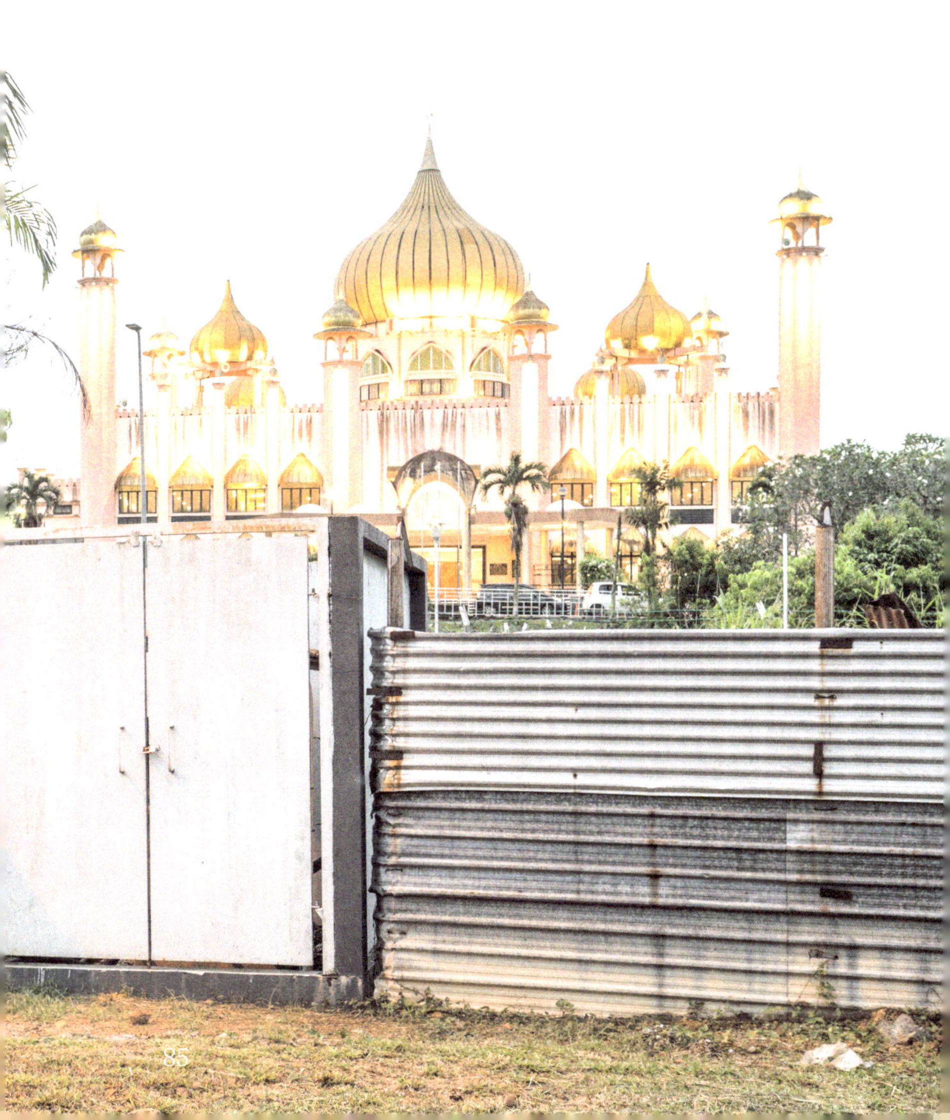

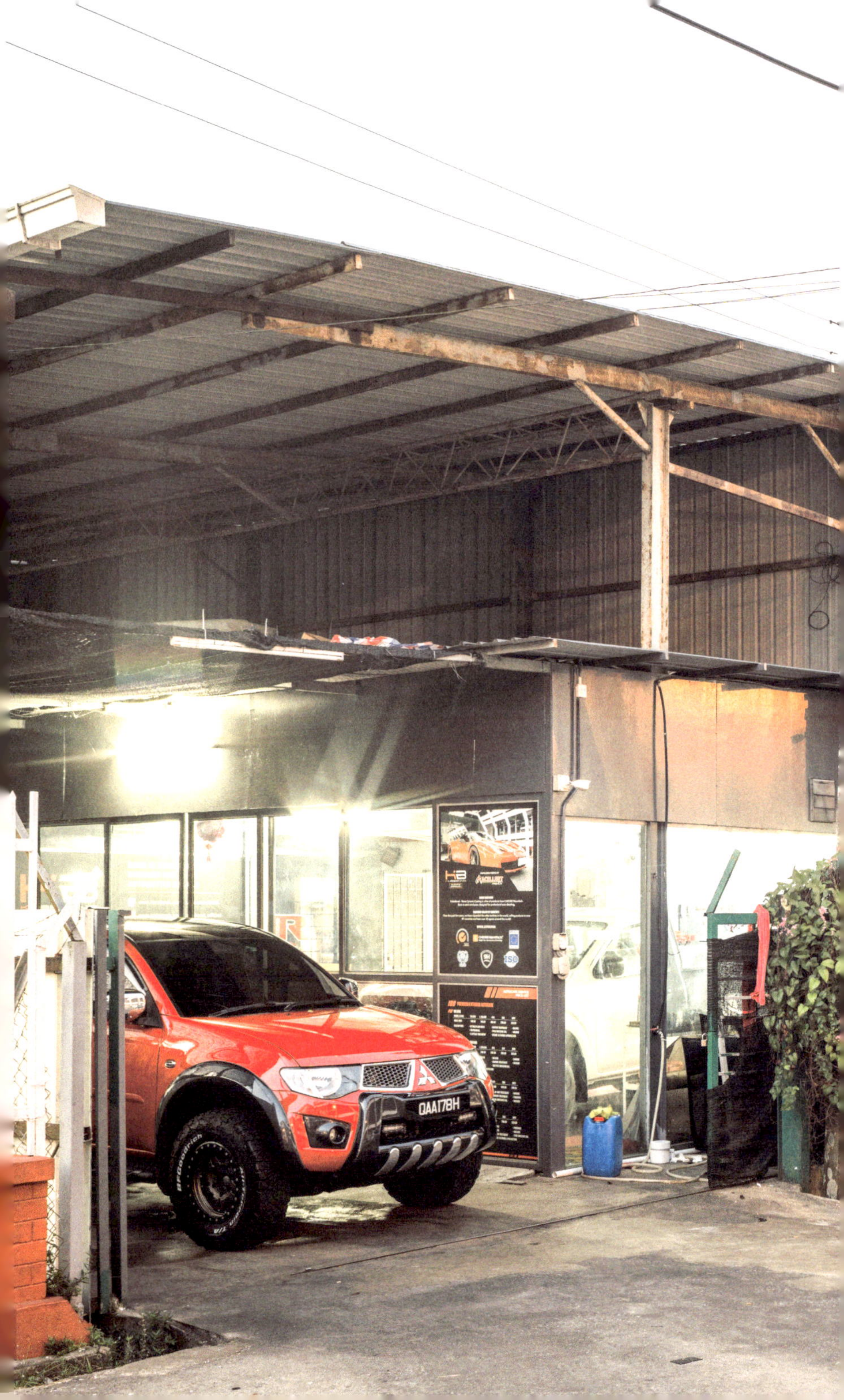
QAA178H

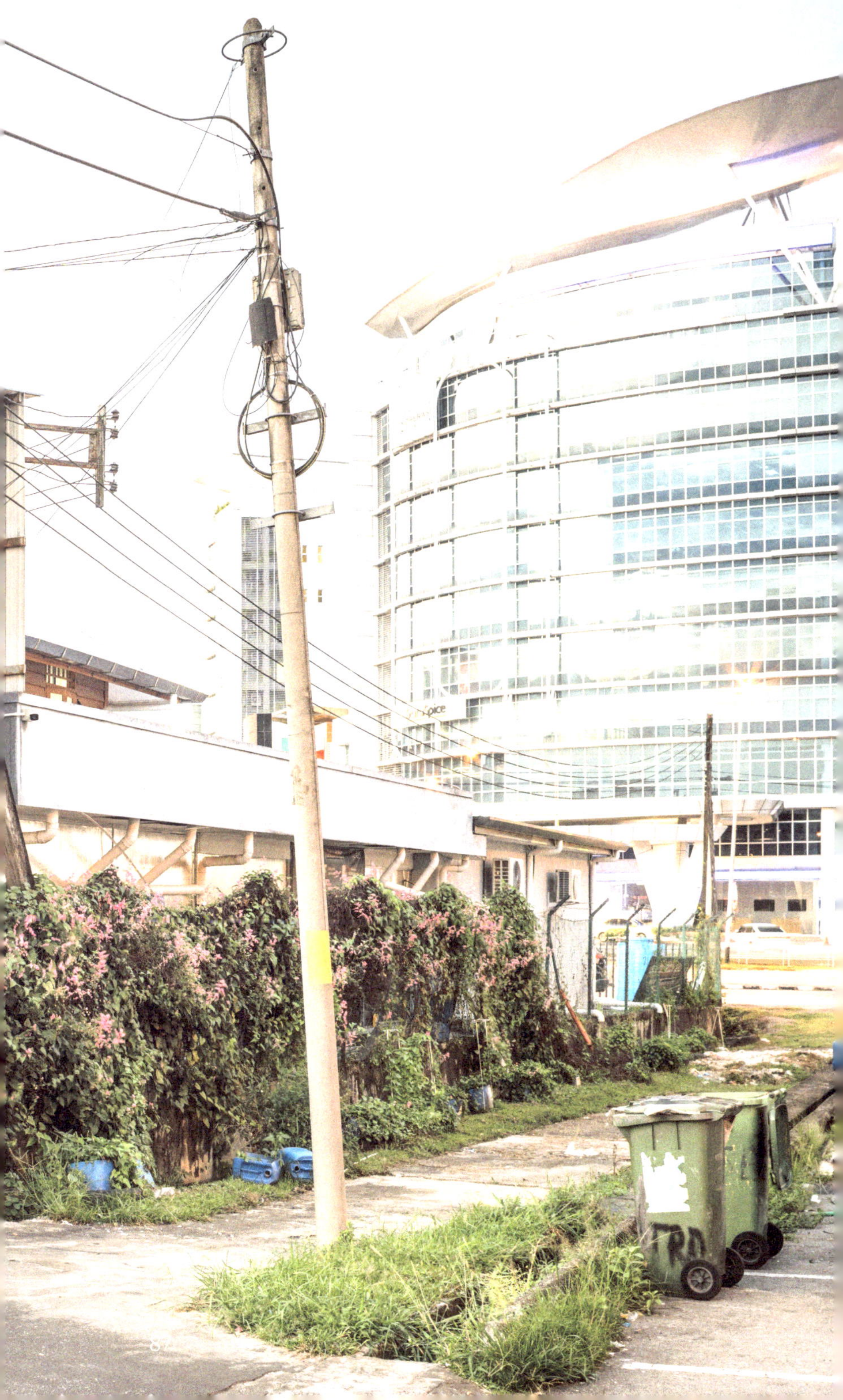

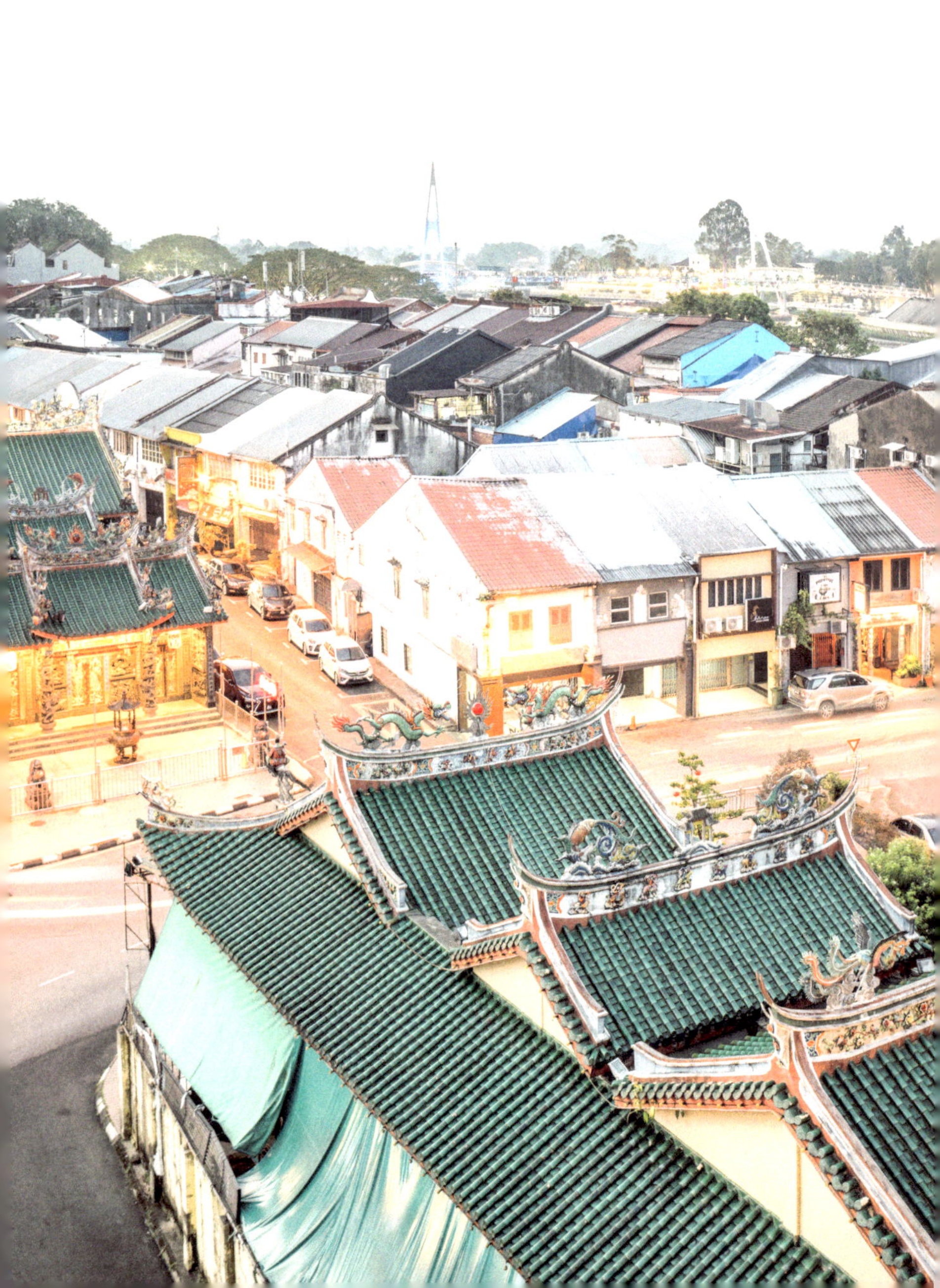

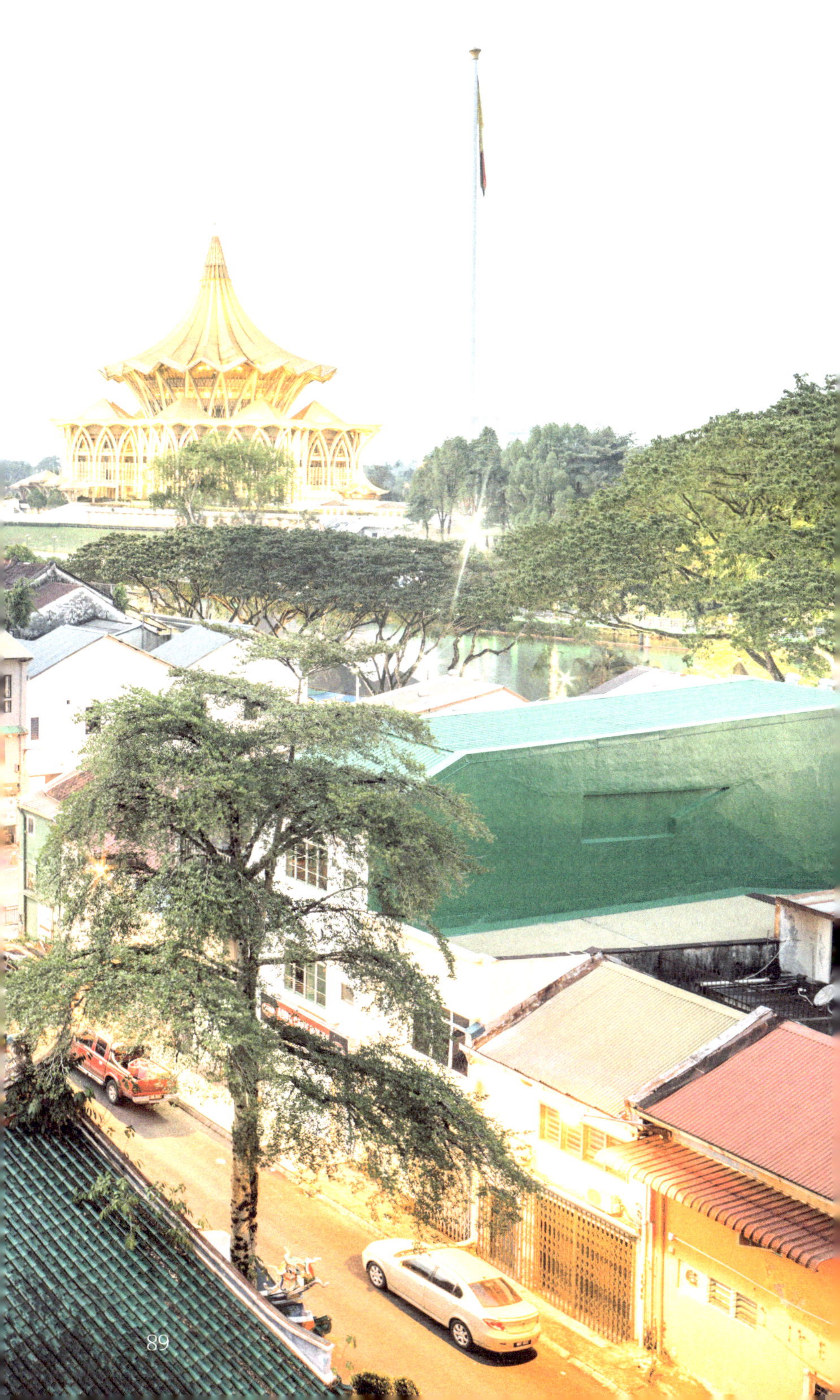

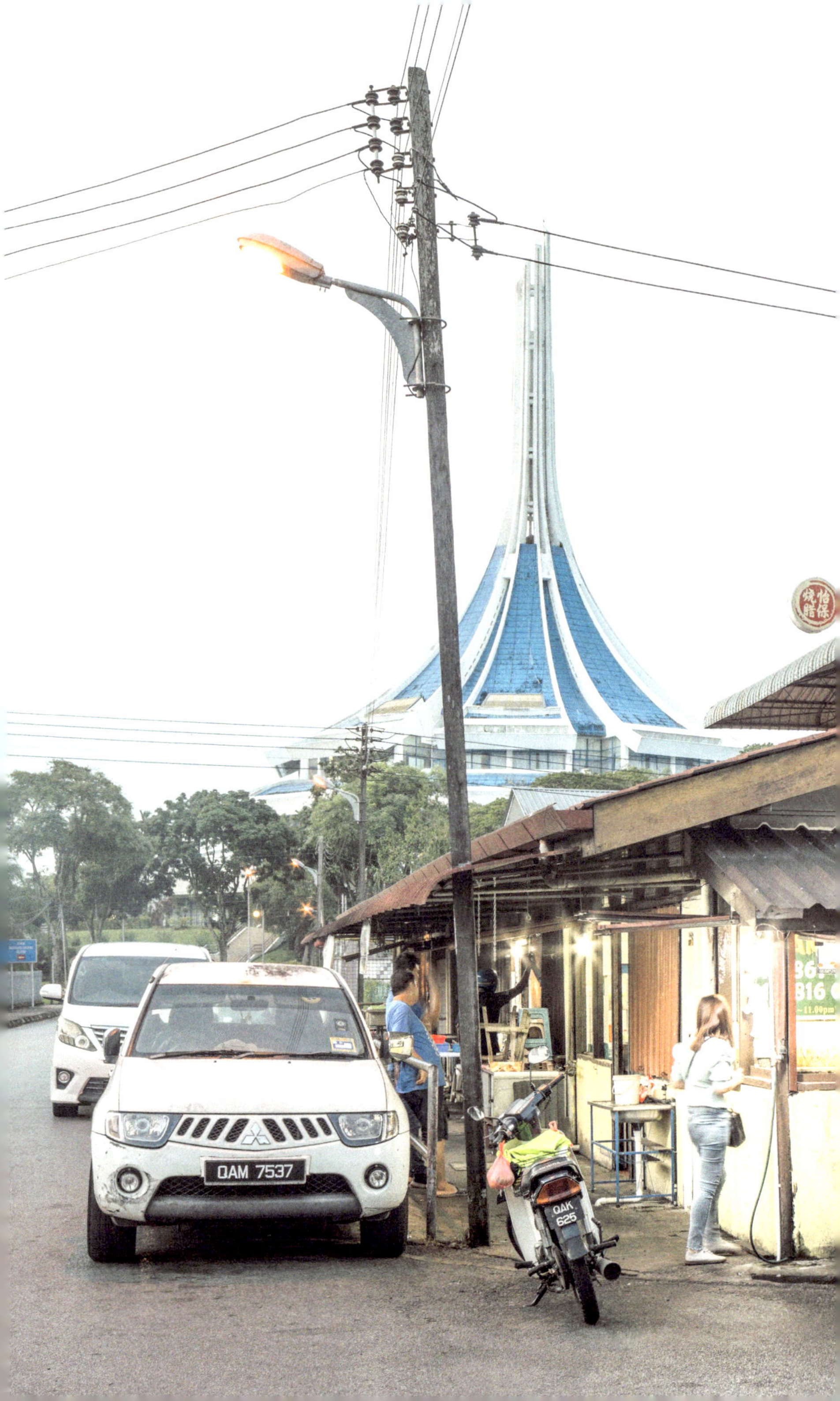
怡保烧腊
QAM 7537
QAK
625

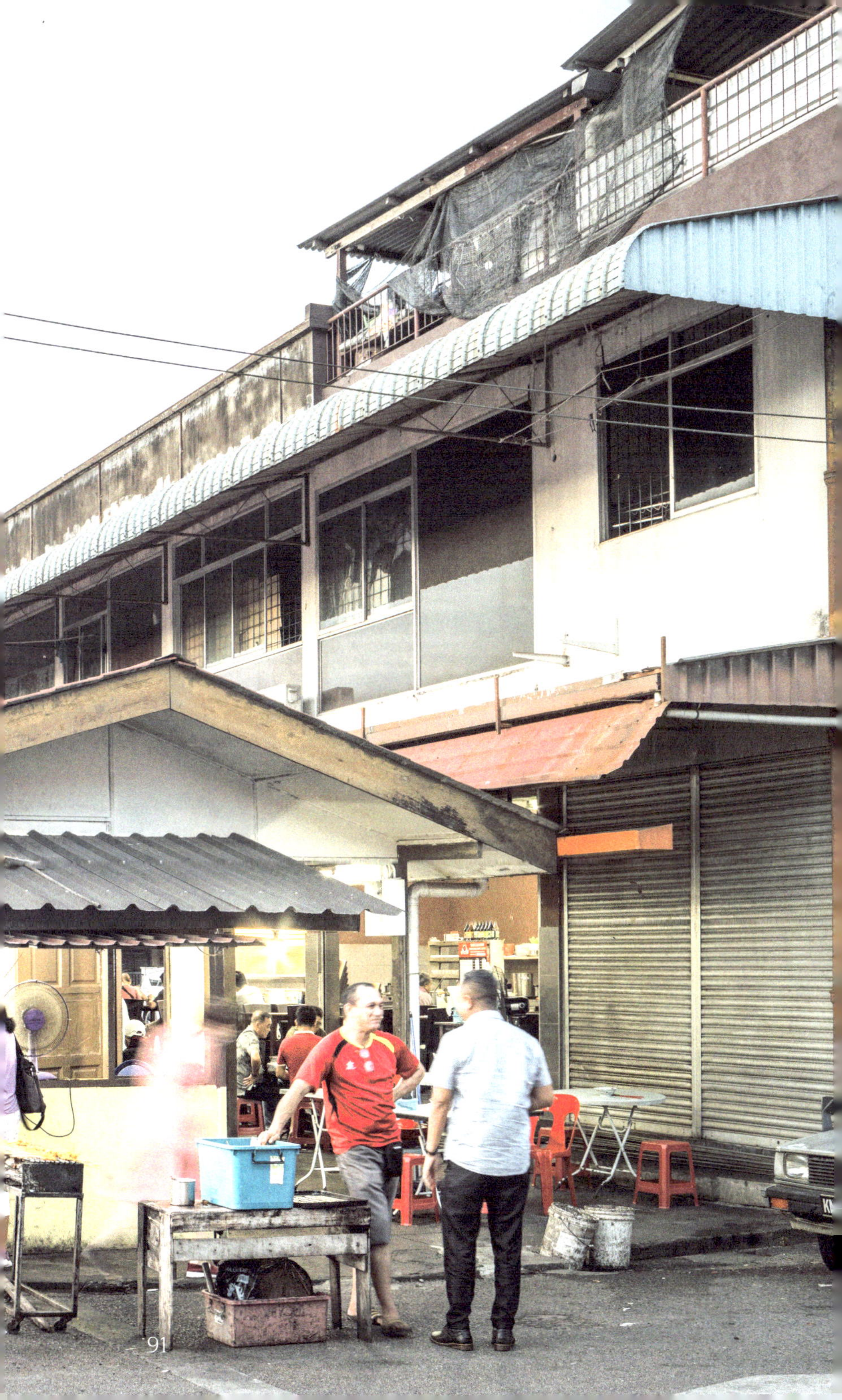

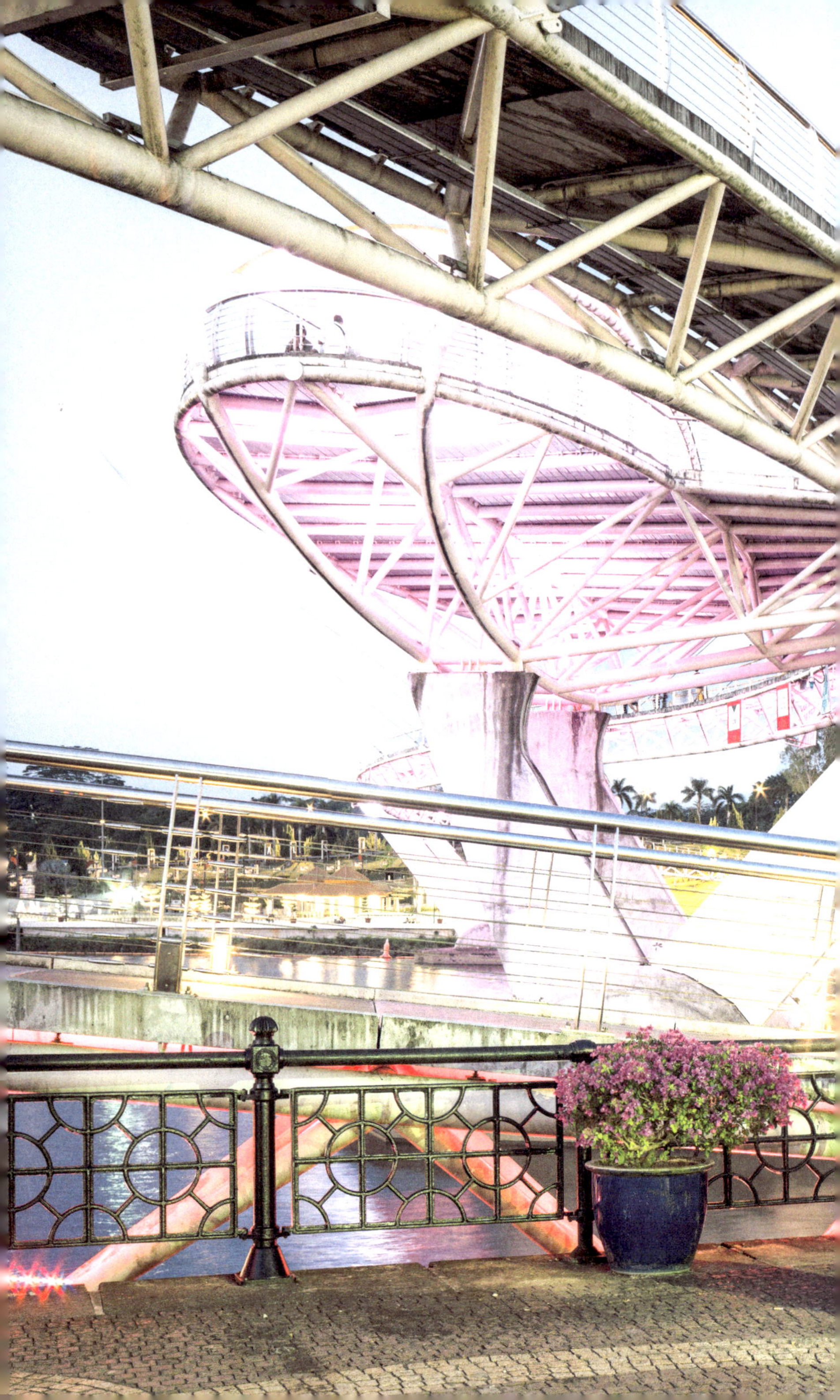

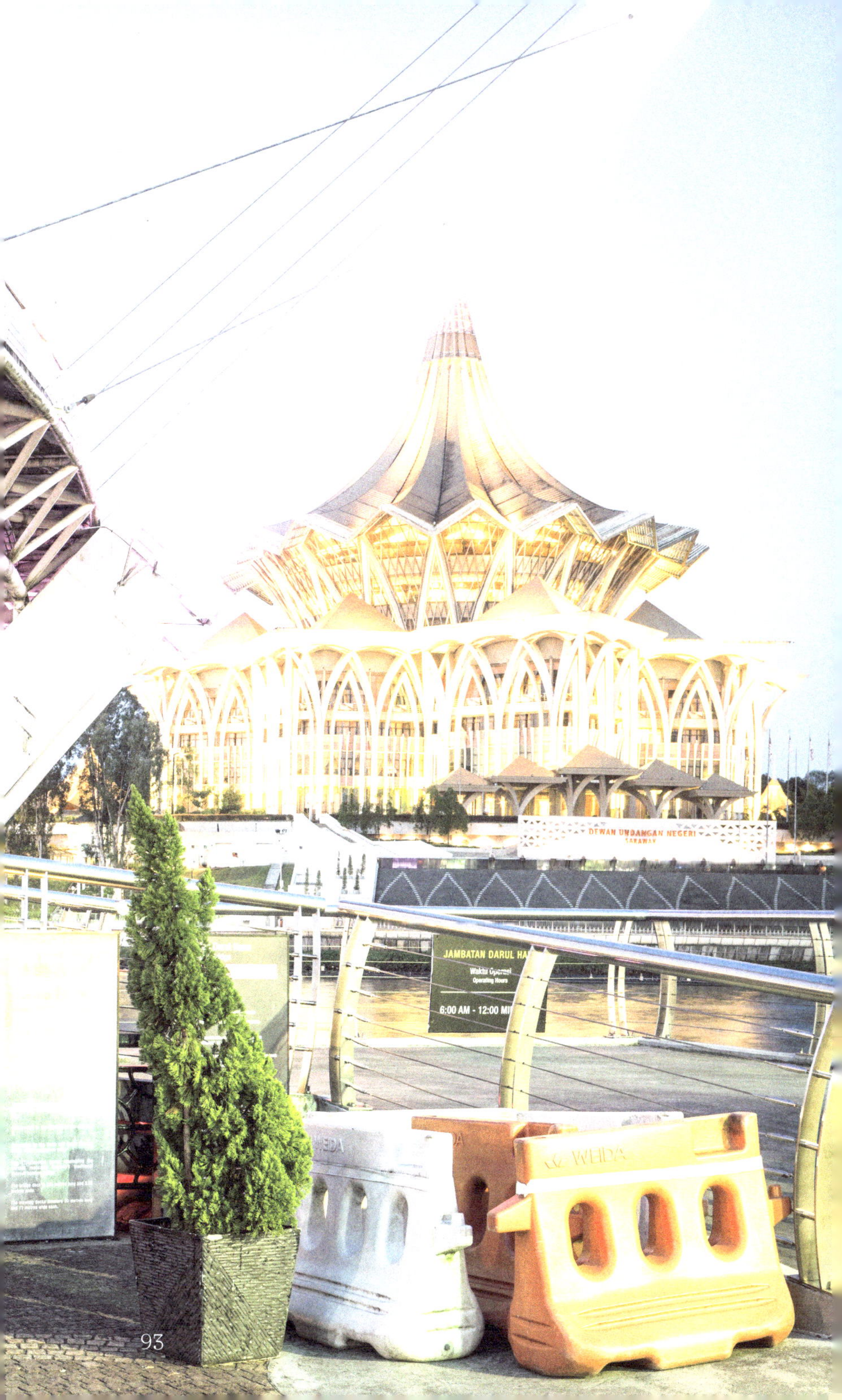
DEWAN UNDANGAN NEGERI
JAMBATAN DARUL HA
Operating Hours
6:00 AM - 12:00 MI
WEIDA

Previous Diaries

Cairo Diary #1
2014
ISBN 978-1-908889-20-1

Athens Diary #2
2015
ISBN 978-1-908889-29-4

Wolfsburg Diary #3
2016
ISBN 978-1-908889-34-8

Taipei Diary #4
2015
ISBN 978-1-908889-30-0

Kochi Diary #5
2018
ISBN 978-1-908889-44-7

Beirut Diary #6
2018
ISBN 978-1-908889-40-9

Wuhan Diary #7
2018
ISBN 978-1-908889-645

Zurich Diary #8
2019
ISBN 978-1-908889-65-2

Budapest Diary #9
2020
ISBN 978-1-908889-66-9

Osaka Diary #10
2020
ISBN 978-1-908889-56-0

Dhaka Diary #11
2021
ISBN 978-1-908889-86-7

Yangon Diary #12
2021
ISBN 978-1-908889-87-4

Minsk Diary #13
2021
ISBN 978-1-908889-88-1

Belfast Diary #14
2021
ISBN 978-1-908889-89-8

Linz Diary #15
2021
ISBN 978-1-908889-90-4

The previous diaries have been publis-hed by *thevelvetcell.com* and are availa-ble through the website.

George Town Diary #16
2022
ISBN 978-3-96070-090-6

Unna Diary #17
2022
ISBN 978-3-96070-089-0

Sarajevo Diary #18
2022
ISBN 978-3-96070-088-3

Bangkok Diary #19
2022
ISBN 978-3-96070-087-6

Kuching Diary #20
2024
ISBN 978-3-96070 105 7

Turin Diary #21
2024
ISBN 978-3-96070-103-3

Wilson Diary #22
2024
ISBN 978-3-96070-106-4

London Diary #23
2024
ISBN 978-3-96070-104-0

Kuching Diary
Peter Bialobrzeski

Published by
Hartmann Books
Liststraße 28/1
70180 Stuttgart
hartmann-books.com

Photographs
Peter Bialobrzeski
bialobrzeski.net

Graphic Design and Typesetting
Sarah Fricke, Distaff Studio

Copyediting
Tas Skorupa, New York

Printing and Binding
DZA Druckerei zu Altenburg

Paper
Pergraphica Natural Rough

Typefaces
ABC Diatype, GT Alpina

First Edition, 2024
500

ISBN
978-3-96070-105-7

For Michael

This project is kindly supported by
Goethe-Institut Malaysia